Don't rush through this book; it should be savored bit by bit; here is exposition one can chew on. You can bask in its fresh insights (Why didn't I think of it that way?), treasure its obvious sympathy (for faith in its bleakness and despair), squirm under its searching exposure (Do we really recognize our idolatry?)—and all the while Dr Ross keeps you firmly tethered to Jesus. Here is a mind-filling, soul-nourishing, Christ-focused feast!

Dale Ralph Davis
Minister in Residence, First Presbyterian Church, Columbia, South Carolina

Those who are acquainted with Philip Ross' fine doctoral work, *From the Finger of God*, already know what a careful scholar, student and expositor he is. The same values are evident in the present book.

Whether he is tackling the often ticklish questions of the relation of the 'Egyptian Hallel' to early Jewish Passover liturgies or the (plainly more congenial) task of exposition of the Psalms we meet with the same painstaking care, attention to detail, mastery of facts and subject, and, above all, devout recognition of Holy Scripture as the Word of God. The whole book is equally illuminating and heart-warming.

Alec Motyer (1924–2016)
Commentator & Old Testament Scholar

Philip Ross combines literary skill, historical breadth, academic depth, and timely wit in encouraging the psalms for 'a later age,' that is, for the church today. He gives due consideration to their original setting for the Old Testament church, to their meaning for Jesus in the Upper Room, and for the Christian church. Ross' exposition will prove profitable for students of Scripture, and particularly for those seeking deeper insight into Jesus' experience in the last hours of his earthly ministry.

Senior Pastor, Independ

To be a Christian is to believe and trust in the atoning sacrifice of Christ. Yet what few Christians realize is that this passion of Christ, even the very words Christ prayed during his agony, are drawn from the psalms, specifically Psalms 113–118. With pastoral care and sobering conviction, Philip Ross reveals why these psalms became our Savior's dying anthem. The reason why should move every reader to his or her knees in worship, praising God for the salvation he has accomplished through his Son, the Lamb of God.

MATTHEW BARRETT
Associate Professor of Christian Theology,
Midwestern Baptist Theological Seminary, Kansas City, Missouri

Jewish scholars long ago realised that Psalms 113–118 form a significant grouping within the Psalter. Because these psalms were part of the Passover liturgy has suggested to Christian scholars that they formed the content of what Jesus and his disciples sang after the first Lord's Supper (Matt. 26:30). Philip Ross expounds these psalms with particular reference to the Messiah's probable use of them. In many respects his presentation resembles that of Dr Klaas Schilder in the first volume of his famous trilogy, *Christ in His Suffering*, in which he entitles his discussion on them, 'The Author Sings His Own Psalms'. One doesn't have to agree with all of the exegesis in this book to enjoy and benefit from its lively, challenging, and deeply spiritual presentation. Read and ponder the implications of the Dying Lamb facing Calvary in the light of these songs that extol God's power to save.

ALLAN M. HARMAN
Research Professor of Old Testament,
Presbyterian Theological College, Melbourne, Australia

PHILIP S. ROSS

ANTHEMS *for a* DYING LAMB

paperback ISBN 978-1-5271-0087-9
epub ISBN 978-1-5271-0127-2
mobi ISBN 978-1-5271-0128-9

Published by
Christian Focus Publications Ltd,
Geanies House,
Fearn, Ross-shire, IV20 1TW, Scotland, UK

www.christianfocus.com

Cover design by Paul Lewis

Printed by Bell & Bain, Glasgow

PHILIP S. ROSS

ANTHEMS *for a* DYING LAMB

How Six Psalms (113–118)
Became a Songbook for the Last Supper
and the Age to Come

CHRISTIAN
FOCUS

For Joan Kerr,

Geraldine MacLennan, and Fiona Rennie.

Contents

Introduction

Scaffold Psalmody

Angers, 1556. Jean Rabec lost his tongue—physically and irrecoverably. This loss he suffered, not through carelessness or disease, but at the hand of Roman Catholic bishops, hell-bent on stopping him singing. Not that sixteenth century bishops enacted brutal punishments on anyone who sang off-key. Their problem with Rabec went beyond his choral capabilities to matters more spiritual, specifically his Huguenot convictions, for which he would shortly burn at the stake. This might make his total glossectomy seem a pointless procedure, but the bishops judged it a critical intervention because when Protestant martyrs went to the stake singing, spectators would turn into a congregation, united with the dying Christian in his final doxology.

Jean Rabac, however, could not be silenced. He would sing without his tongue, even if his words were recognisable only to those who knew Marot's Psalms—

Les gens entrez son ten ton héritage;
Ils ont pollu, seigneur, par leur outrage...

Ô Dieu Sauveur, pour l'amour de ta glorie,
Pour conserver de ton nom la mémoire,
Regarde-nous avec des yeux propices,
Et sauve-nous malgré nos injustices...

Or, in a more vulgar tongue:

O God, the nations have come into your inheritance;
they have defiled your holy temple ...

Help us, O God of our salvation,
for the glory of your name;
deliver us, and atone for our sins,
for your name's sake! (Psa. 79:1, 9 ESV)

And he kept singing until the flames overcame him.[1]

The Huguenots did not invent such scaffold psalmody, and nor did it disappear with their persecution. In the fourth century, Theodore the Recruit died for his Christian faith, perhaps in part because he chose to express it by burning down a pagan temple. In a homily to commemorate Theodore's accelerated martyrdom, Gregory of Nyssa recounts how during the holy arsonist's prolonged execution he sang 'a verse of a psalm: "I will praise the Lord on every occasion, his praise is always in my mouth" (Ps. 33:2) [34:1]. They tore most of his flesh in pieces, he was singing psalms as if somebody else was undergoing the

1 Rowland E. Prothero, *The Psalms in Human Life* (London: John Murray, 1905), 193.

torture.'[2] Even in nineteenth century Scotland, when two men, John Baird and Andrew Hardie, were hanged and beheaded in Stirling for a cause more political than religious, they sang Psalm 51 and Psalm 103, with Hardie almost acting as precentor at his own funeral, 'giving out two lines at a time, in a clear and distinct voice,' before he 'gave the signal when they were launched into eternity.'[3]

Martyrs and malefactors are not the only category to turn to the Psalms at life's close. From the famous poetry of Psalm 23 or Psalm 84, to the less-familiar words of Psalm 17 or Psalm 71, this truly catholic hymnal has been a faithful minster at many 'ordinary' Christian deathbeds, speaking comfortable words to the dying, or expressing longings and convictions, inwrought by years of worship, devotion, and trial. In this, Christians are like their Saviour who had the Psalms on his lips as he laid down his life. Two of his seven sayings on the cross, and all of his citations from Scripture as he hung abandoned, came from the Psalms: 'My God, my God, why have you forsaken me?' (Matt. 27:46) from Psalm 22, and 'Father, into your hands, I commit my spirit' (Luke 23:46) from Psalm 31. His last words took shape not in a moment of death's confusion, but during a life saturated in the language and robust piety of the Psalms—piety he embraced through hearing, reading, or recitation, and also in singing. The musical forms and melodies of Jesus' day remain somewhat mysterious, yet Jesus surely did sing. Even in the last twenty-four hours of his life, he sang. The Gospels

2 Johan Leemans, Wendy Mayer, Pauline Allen and Boudewijn Dehandschutter, *'Let Us Die that We May Live': Greek Homilies on Christian Martyrs from Asia Minor, Palestine and Syria (c. AD 350–AD 450)*, (London: Routledge, 2003), 89.

3 *A Full, True, and Particular Account of the Execution of Andrew Hardie and John Baird: Who Were Hanged and Beheaded at Stirling, on Friday the 8th September 1820, for High Treason with Their Behaviour at the Place of Execution* (Edinburgh: William Cameron, 1820).

record that after Jesus had given the cup to his disciples, and before they went out to the Mount of Olives, they 'sung a hymn' (Matt. 26:30; Mark 14:26), almost universally reckoned to be Psalm 118, or some portion of Psalms 113–118, which we know as 'The Egyptian Hallel'. Like many who would take up their cross and follow him, Jesus sang Psalms as death approached, specifically Psalms 113–118. These were the last songs of Jesus.

This book is about those six Psalms, which chapters 3–8 will consider in turn. Should you choose to skip the next two chapters, or decide to read them later, chapters 3–8 should still make sense, but their content does presuppose certain conclusions found in chapters 1–2:

- Chapter 1 sets out the reasons for seeing a connection between the Hallel and Passover.
- Chapter 2 is about attitudes to the Psalms and their interpretation. If parts of it appear technical, that does not signal the complexity of chapters 3–8. It is because I wish to explain why the Psalms are songs 'for a later age' and to interact with discussions that may interest those who wish to study background issues. Doing that in a separate chapter seemed preferable to a blizzard of explanatory footnotes in chapters 3–8. It also means that all footnotes in this book are for reference only.

In chapters 3–8 those references highlight some distinctive contributions to the study of Psalms 113–118 and other works from which I have benefited. I am most indebted, however, to the ordinary preachers and Christians whose Psalm-infused Christocentricity shaped my thinking during my childhood, long before I consciously thought about the Psalms.

Finally, I will also keep references to the biblical languages to a minimum, but it may be obvious when some point or other is dependent on an observable feature in the Hebrew text.

1

Passover Praise?

Can we be sure that Psalms 113–118 were the last songs of Jesus? After all, the Gospels do not provide a footnote saying 'i.e. the Egyptian Hallel, Psalms 113–118.' I could back up this claim with my own footnote, citing twenty-four commentators and scholars, ancient and modern, all of whom think the Gospels refer to those Psalms. One of them, however, could be making a baseless assumption, while the remaining twenty-three cite the first as their authority, so we should test the claim ourselves.

The Last Passover

The first question we need to ask is, what kind of meal was the Last Supper? Was it obviously a Passover meal? If Jesus sent his disciples to prepare the Passover (Matt. 26:18–19; Mark 14:13–16; Luke 22:8–13), what else could it be? If he reclined at the table with his apostles and said to them, 'I have longed to eat this Passover with you before I suffer' (Luke 22:15), could that meal be something other than a Passover celebration? For some, John's Gospel is decisive:

'the Last Supper did not occur on the night the Passover was celebrated.'[1] Certainly, John 13:1 begins with the words, 'Now before the Feast of the Passover,' and during Jesus' trial, the Jews had yet to 'eat the Passover' (John 18:28), but was John really in a different time zone (at least until 'the first day of the week')? Whoever has the patience may familiarise themselves with a catalogue of works surrounding this, the New Testament's 'most disputed calendric question,'[2] but when even those who think the 'Last Supper' took place before Passover admit the meal 'had Passover characteristics,'[3] such patience may be a doubtful virtue. Whatever one concludes about a supposed conflict between John and the other Gospel writers, dates and calendars cannot settle the question. After the first Passover in Egypt, the date did not make the meal; the meal made the date. A Passover meal did not need to be consumed on the fourteenth day of the first month for it to be a Passover meal (Num. 9:6–12)—something Hezekiah and his princely counsellors well understood (2 Chron. 30:1–5). Even so, we need not suppose that Hezekiah's most famous son celebrated Passover a day early. It is possible, as Andreas Köstenberger shows, to present a level-headed case for John's account being in alignment with the other Gospels.[4] 'Proposed historical, theological, and canonical inconsistencies...prove lacking under close scrutiny.'[5] A straightforward reading of Matthew,

1 Robert Letham, *The Lord's Supper: Eternal Word in Broken Bread* (Phillipsburg: P&R, 2001), 4.

2 Raymond E. Brown, *The Gospel According to John (xiii–xxi)*, (New York: Doubleday, 1978), 555. Brown lists several works (556), as does Jane S. Webster, *Ingesting Jesus: Eating and Drinking in the Gospel of John* (Lieden: Brill, 2003), 102.

3 Brown, *John*, 556.

4 Andreas J. Köstenberger, 'Was the Last Supper a Passover Meal?' in Thomas R. Schreiner & Matthew R. Crawford (eds.), *The Lord's Supper: Remembering and Proclaiming Christ Until He Comes* (Nashville: B&H Publishing Group, 2001), 6–30.

5 Ibid., 29–30.

Mark, and Luke is not touching naivety: the Last Supper was a Passover meal.[6]

'And When They Had Sung a Hymn'

That brings us to the main issue, the 'hymn' of Matthew 26 and Mark 14. Why should we think that hymn was Psalm 118, or a part of the Egyptian Hallel—Psalms 113–118? Indisputably, these Psalms have, to this day, been associated with the celebration of Passover. During the Seder, a festival meal held in Jewish homes on the first evening of the Passover holiday, a book called the *Hagaddah* directs proceedings. Shortly after retelling the Passover story, the leader raises the second cup, and after some words of thanksgiving says, 'Let us then sing a new song,' which leads into Psalms 113–114.[7] As the celebration moves into the final part, the fourth cup is poured and they open the door for Elijah, hoping to see Malachi 4:5 fulfilled. Then, having called upon God to pour out his wrath upon those that do not call on his name, they recite Psalms 115–118,[8] usually singing verses 21–24 of Psalm 118 twice: 'the stone which the builders rejected has become the corner stone.'[9]

But how ancient is this practice? What if, as some argue, the Seder and *Haggadah* are 'the creative response of rabbis in the

6 See also Routledge: 'the Last Supper (whether or not celebrated a day early) had the character of a Passover meal.' Robin Routledge, 'Passover and the Last Supper,' *Tyndale Bulletin* 53.2 (2002), 222. Marcus also argues against challenges 'from scholars of ancient Judaism rather than NT specialists.' They 'overemphasize the biblical [OT] and rabbinic evidence and downplay or ignore evidence from the book of *Jubilees*, Philo, and especially the NT.' Joel Marcus, 'Passover and Last Supper Revisited,' *New Testament Studies* 59.3 (2013), 304, 307.

7 Chaim Raphael, *A Feast of History: The drama of Passover through the ages with a new translation of the Haggadah for use at the Seder* (London & Jerusalem: Weidenfeld and Nicolson, 1972), 50 [207].

8 Ibid., 67 [190].

9 Ibid., 71 [186].

second century to the destruction of the Temple'[10] and New Testament commentators are now reading post-70 AD Judaic traditions back into the Gospel narratives? It takes little reading of Jewish discussion about the *Haggadah* to discover that, as with most ancient texts and customs, someone has always been willing to dispute over details, such as the colour of the wine to be used, or how much leaning to the left is required.[11] Despite such debate, however, the Seder as Judaism practices it today took its final form at the beginning of the second century, and some of its content stretches back to 200 BC.[12] In addition, the *Haggadah* is not the only source to associate the Hallel with Passover; the *Mishnah* does likewise. This second century 'crown jewel of Rabbinic Judaism,'[13] records the sayings of Judaic authorities, most of whom lived between 70 and 200 AD,[14] yet it ascribes to itself effectively-divine authority:

> Tractate Abot records the origins of the Mishnah's traditions in a chain of tradition beginning with God's revelation of the Torah to Moses at Sinai...and continuing through specified figures who received and handed on the same tradition. The list of names ends up with sages important in the Mishnah itself...who through a process of discipleship transmit an essential part of the revelation of the Torah at Sinai.[15]

10 Joshua Kulp, 'The Origins of the Seder and Haggadah,' *Currents in Biblical Research* 4.1 (2005), 129.

11 Isaac Levy, *A Guide to Passover* (London: Jewish Chronicle Publications, 1958), 53–5.

12 Raphael, *Feast of History*, 67.

13 Jacob Neusner, *Making God's Word Work: A Guide to the Mishnah* (New York: Continuum, 2004), 11.

14 *The Mishnah: A New Translation*, trans. Jacob Neusner (New Haven: Yale University Press, 1988), xvi.

15 Neusner, *Making God's Word Work*, 33.

What we read in the *Mishnah* therefore carries great weight as a description of what second century Judaism understood to be the most ancient practice. Peshaim 5:7 describes proceedings during the slaughter of the Passover lamb at the Temple:

> [The Levites meanwhile] proclaimed the Hallel psalms [113–118]. If they completed [the recitation], they repeated it, and if they completed the second time, they repeated it for a third—even though they never in all their days had to repeat it for a third time. R. Judah says, 'In all the days of the third group they never even reached the verse, I love the Lord because he has heard my voice (Ps. 116:1) because its numbers were small.'[16]

Even those rabbinic scholars who may not share the *Mishnah*'s lofty self-evaluation still consider the Hallel to be an original element of Passover celebrations.[17] It was one of the 'two main components' during the time of the Temple.[18] The lack of a pre-Christian manuscript containing the *Haggadah,* or the *Mishnah*'s Passover liturgy, does not mean we must retreat from the idea that the Hallel was sung at Passover. The 'entire liturgy was orally delivered,' so we should not expect to find an original text.[19] This combination of oral tradition and its second century transcription makes it reasonable to conclude that when extra-biblical writings, or Philo,[20] or in our case the New

16 *Mishnah*, trans. Neusner.

17 Joseph Tabory, 'Towards a History of the Paschal Meal' in *Two Liturgical Traditions (Vol. 5), Passover and Easter: Origin and History to Modern Times*, Paul F. Bradshaw and Lawrence A. Hoffman (eds.) (Notre Dame: University of Notre Dame Press, 1999), 64.

18 Israel J. Yuval, 'Early Jewish-Christian Dialogue' in Bradshaw and Lawrence, *Two Liturgical Traditions*, 105, 113.

19 Lawrence A. Hoffman, 'The Passover Meal in Jewish Tradition' in Bradshaw and Lawrence, *Two Liturgical Traditions*, 13.

20 J. B. Segal, *The Hebrew Passover: From the Earliest Times to A.D. 70* (London: Oxford University Press, 1963), 22, 25–6, 30.

Testament, refer to Passover psalms or hymns, Psalms 113–118 are in view. In fact, our basis for understanding the 'hymn' of Matthew 26 and Mark 14 as a reference to the Hallel is more secure than the basis for many widely-accepted scholarly claims about the meaning and context of biblical passages, not least concerning the Psalms. That is to say, we may be hugely more confident that Jesus sang Psalms 113–118 at the Last Supper than, for example, that Psalm 24 was composed for an Israelite enthronement festival. Based on textual and historical evidence, the former is beyond reasonable doubt; the latter is speculation donned in scholarly respectability.[21]

But what of the original Old Testament context of the Hallel Psalms? Were they written for a specific setting? Gunkel and Kraus judged Psalm 114 'best suited to Passover,'[22] which is as tame an observation as suggesting that Genesis 1 deals with creation. Goulder is more adventurous: Psalm 115 'was written to be part of the Passover liturgy, and it has remained a part of it ever since'[23]—for him, just one block in an elaborate reconstruction, which sees the returned exiles of Ezra 6:19–22 celebrating Passover 'with a sequence of fourteen psalms, 105–118, of which the odd numbers were used in the evening, and the even numbers in the morning.'[24] By comparison, Zenger's comment on the Hallel's setting is mercifully brief: 'it was put together as a liturgical cantata by Temple singers' and 'sung in choir during the great pilgrimage feasts in the Temple.'[25]

21 For an account of interpretative approaches to the Psalms see Bruce K. Waltke & James M. Houston, *The Psalms in Christian Worship: A Historical Commentary* (Grand Rapids: Eerdmans, 2010), 37–79, esp. 75–77; also Derek Kidner, *Psalms 1–72* (Leicester: Inter-Varsity Press, 1973), 7–18.

22 Michael D. Goulder, *The Psalms of the Return (Book V, Psalms 107–150)* (Sheffield: Sheffield Academic Press, 1988), 166.

23 Ibid., 174.

24 Ibid., 209.

25 Frank-Lohar Hossfeld and Erich Zenger, *Psalms 3: A Commentary on Psalms 101–150*, trans. Linda M. Maloney (Minneapolis: Fortress Press, 2011), 179.

Even if these conjectures contain enough grains of truth to make a reasonable case, the Hallel Psalms give no explicit indication that they first appeared under the title *Passover Praise*. Were they grouped together in the Psalter especially for that purpose, or were they put to that use later? So far, nobody knows. And what the Psalter chooses not to tell us about the original setting, we probably do not need to know. It is certainly a united and coherent compilation—a deliberate grouping, not an accidental assortment. The collection falls into two parts.[26]

	Corporate	Personal
Praise & Thanksgiving	113	116
Call to the Nations	114	117
Praise & Thanksgiving	115	118

Psalms 113–115 call us to praise the LORD together, united in worship and thankfulness for his love. Psalms 116–118 become more personal, although not exclusively. While in 113–115, the psalmist never says, 'I', 'me', or 'my', in 116–118 he says 'I', 'me', or 'my', 72 times. This is not a slide into pietistic narcissism; when God saves his people, his salvation becomes personal. Both sets of outer Psalms (113 and 115, 116 and 118) are songs of praise and thanksgiving, while the centre Psalms (114 and 117) call on the nations to worship. Repeated words and phrases, many 'Hallelujahs', stitch the two parts into one theme of praise and expectation—a unanimous exhortation to people of all nations to exit bondage and embrace the LORD's redeeming reign.

26 See Zenger's detailed, scholarly expression of this structure, ibid., 178–9. An alternative approach sees Psalm 117 as the 'discourse peak': Elizabeth Hayes, 'The Unity of the Egyptian Hallel: Psalms 113–18,' *Bulletin for Biblical Research* 9.1 (1999), 150. On the unusual difficulty of even demarcating individual poems in the Hallel see Gert T. M. Prinsloo, 'Unit Delimitations in the Egyptian Hallel (Psalms 113–118): An Evaluation of Different Traditions' in *Unit Delimitation in Biblical Hebrew and Northwest Semitic Literature* (ed. Marjo C. A. Korpel and Josef M. Oesch; Pericope 4; Assen: Van Gorcum, 2003), 232–65.

It is therefore not surprising that Psalms 113–118 became a fixed element in the Passover liturgy. What these Psalms do tell us allow us to make sense of the Hallel, and to show why sometime in the centuries before Christ, it became the 'hymn' for Passover. When Christians celebrated the Lord's Supper that association continued. Ancient writers, such as Chrysostom and Augustine, record the use of the Hallel, particularly Psalm 118, during weekly worship, or at Easter[27]—a practice preserved in East and West over the centuries.[28] Even when the celebration of the sacrament became less frequent in the post-Reformation Western Church, the Eucharist and the Hallel stayed together. In the Reformed churches of Scotland, Psalm 116 was an almost-fixed element of the communion service, while the Hallel Psalms remain a regular constituent of some Anglican liturgies for Easter, sometimes interwoven with Jesus' last discourse and prayer (John 13:31–17:26).

For many Western Christians, however, Psalms will not even make it into a communion service. Evangelicalism in particular has almost completely displaced these hymns and songs of Scripture. Why, when Rabec lost his tongue, yet kept singing Psalms, have modern Christians kept their tongues, but lost their Psalters? Setting aside trivial reasons, such as the abominable quality of some congregational singing, or the impenetrable verse in certain Psalters, the most likely reason is that today's Christian does not read the Psalms how Rabec read the Psalms. They meant something to him in 1556 that they do not mean to Western Christians today, so we must now ask what has changed and what attempts have been made to reset current attitudes to the Psalms.

27 James W. McKinnon, *The Advent Project: The Later-seventeenth century Creation of the Roman Mass Proper* (Berkeley: University of California Press, 2000), 48, 52, 274.

28 Michael Farrow, *Psalm Verses of the Orthodox Liturgy: According to the Greek and Slav Usages* (Torrance: Oakwood Publications, 1997), 32, 112.

2

Songs for a Later Age

The church's neglect of its 'original hymnbook' is, according N. T. Wright, 'a great impoverishment'—nothing less than 'crazy'.[1] By comparison, Waltke and Houston's similar observation has all the passion of an autopsy report: 'Since the eighteenth century, hymnody has replaced the centrality of the Psalter in the liturgy of evangelical churches.'[2] Yet those varied authors are united in their desire to see the church 'recover these losses,'[3] restoring the Psalms to Christian worship, and not just to the 'vaguely pious use of them'[4] that followed the eighteenth-century hymn-writing movement. 'The Psalms

1 N. T. Wright, *The Case for the Psalms: Why They Are Essential* (New York, Harper One: 2013), 5.

2 Bruce K. Waltke & James M. Houston with Erika Moore, *The Psalms as Christian Worship: A Historical Commentary* (Grand Rapids: William B Eerdmans, 2010), 10.

3 Ibid, 11.

4 Ibid., 78.

represent the Bible's own spiritual root system for the great tree we call Christianity. You don't have to be a horticultural genius to know what will happen to the fruit on the tree if the roots are not in good condition.'[5]

If by this point, three centuries of hymn-writers and their promoters have taken sore umbrage at the implication that their songs may produce sub-Christian fruit, they will be in no mood to listen to Wright's claim that 'As you sing the Psalms ...you will be drawn into a world where God and Jesus make sense in a way they would not otherwise do.'[6] And some of them, having long suspected that the church did not properly begin until 31 October 1517, will have little patience with Waltke & Houston's insistence on 'hearing the voice of the believing church'—that is interpreting the Psalms without overlooking 'two thousand years of Christian devotion and orthodoxy or "right worship," in the use of the Book of Psalms.'[7] Indeed, the mere notion of 'right worship' is enough to transform some Christians into their prickliest state, especially if they operate with a profound conviction that God has no particular say in how they worship; God can take what he gets. Even those who recognise such a thing as orthodoxy or 'right worship' are not inclined to take lessons from anyone else on what that means. In this cultural ambience, worshipping communities will pay little more attention to Wright and Waltke's coaxing towards the Psalter than to a firm insistence on excluding uninspired songs from worship.[8] But the main reason most attempts to restore or retain the Psalter are in vain, is that they overlook how much the supplanting of psalmody with extra-biblical song was intertwined with other developments.

5 Wright, *Case for the Psalms*, 5.

6 Ibid., 22.

7 Waltke & Houston, *Psalms*, 3.

8 See, for example, R. Scott Clark, *Recovering the Reformed Confession* (Phillipsburg: P&R, 2008), 227–92.

A Major Wind-up

The first development was musical. Despite many attempts to trace the origins of church music, finding Noah's ark might not be much more difficult. If the early church sang at all during her corporate gatherings, the New Testament narratives keep that quiet. Even Paul's references to psalms, hymns, and spiritual songs (Eph. 5:19; Col. 3:16) do not come in the context of an unmistakable reference to public worship. Building on the work of Eduard Norden, twentieth-century scholarship reached the settled conviction that passages such as Colossians 1:15–20 and Philippians 2:6–11 were hymn quotations, but anyone hoping for what became known as form criticism to come to the rescue, will be disappointed. At barely one hundred years old this approach has lost its grip. It is now judged 'extremely difficult' to make 'any positive statement about their hymnic status'—'The default position for analyzing these passages needs to be simply that they are heightened prose as part of a letter.'[9]

With the New Testament proving so unyeilding, those who hesitate to preinvent their own form of worship in its pages might reach out to church history for guidance, but it too can be stubborn. If 'the most common and presumably the earliest form of singing in church was responsorial' with the response just 'a word, such as "Hallelujah" or "Amen," or a verse, such as "His mercy endures forever"',[10] what was the source of this practice? Was Socrates the ecclesiastical historian right to credit it to Ignatius' 'vision of angels hymning in alternate chants

9 Benjamin Edsall and Jennifer R. Strawbridge, 'The Songs we Used to Sing? Hymn "Traditions" and Reception in Pauline Letters,' *Journal for the Study of the New Testament* 37.3 (2015), 306.

10 Everett Ferguson, 'Music' in *Encyclopaedia of Early Christianity: Second Edition* (Abingdon: Routledge, 2010), 788.

the Holy Trinity'?[11] When 'evidence for the congregational singing of hymns is either nonexistent or controversial'[12] for the first four centuries, where did the fourth-century church in Milan learn the antiphonal singing of Psalms—was it from the Syriac church or the synagogue?[13] How could it have been the synagogue if the assumption 'that psalmody flourished in the ancient synagogue is a notion created by liturgical and musical historians'?[14] If it was only in the fourth century that Ephrem the Syrian 'prompted the writing of hymns in Greek,'[15] what were the Greeks singing before that—if they were singing?

Whatever the answers to such questions, and whatever the character of congregational singing during the first centuries of Christianity, one thing is sure—musical instruments did not accompany it. The Church Fathers had a universal antipathy to such pagan innovations.[16] At best, they were spiritually infantile relics of the old covenant. While Eastern Orthodoxy has maintained that antipathy to this day, in the West, organs and musicians began to make a bashful appearance 'only during

11 *The Ecclesiastical History of Socrates* (London: Henry G. Bohn, 1853), 315.

12 William T. Flynn, 'Liturgical Music' in Geoffrey Wainwright & Karen B. Westerfield Tucker eds., *The Oxford History of Christian Worship* (Oxford: Oxford University Press, 2006), 770.

13 Edward Dickinson, *Music in the History of the Western Church* (New York: Charles Scribner's Sons, 1925), 28–9.

14 James W. McKinnon, 'On the Question of Psalmody in the Ancient Synagogue' in Iain Fenlon ed., *Early Music History (vol. 6): Studies in medieval and early modern music* (Cambridge: CUP, 1986), 180–81. See also J. A. Smith, 'The Ancient Synagogue, the Early Church and Singing' in *Music & Letters* (1984) 65.1, 1–16; Regina Randhofer, 'Singing The Songs of Ancient Israel: tacame 'emet and Oral Models as Criteria for Layers Of Time In Jewish Psalmody.' *Journal of Musicological Research* 24:3–4 (2005), 241–64.

15 Diarmaid MacCulloch, *A History of Christianity* (London: Penguin Books, 2010), 183.

16 See James McKinnon, *Music in Early Christian Literature* (Cambridge: Cambridge University Press, 1989).

the high and late Middle Ages (1100–1450).'[17] Yet despite this, and despite the Great Schism of 1054, East and West were still singing in harmony (if one can say that of chant and plainsong). According to McCulloch, 'The real separation came with the trauma of the complete Ottoman conquest in 1453, when a great divergence in musical practice began. In particular, the Orthodox were never seized by the enthusiasm for the pipe organ…'[18] For the Western church, that initial divergence was only the beginning. Apart from a few bouts of apathy, she was seized with an enthusiasm for all things musical that would overflow into unbrotherly passions. No longer would musical divergence follow real separation; it would become the direct cause.

Now, over 500 years later, the woman who sways gently and dewy-eyed to the latest pseudo-Celtic hymnodic kitsch cannot worship with the man who insists on the 'great hymns' (that is Toplady, Wesley, etc.—'They were good enough for Moses …'), and he in turn cannot unite with a traditional Anglican whose statuesque chanting is a sure sign of spiritual death. As for exclusive psalmodists, they happily sing about how good it is to dwell together in unity, but how would they know? Despite being the only people who agree with each other on music and song, they cannot agree on anything else. Seeking to mend the body of Christ, some bold innovators have pursued a great convergence, striving to unite these separated brethren under the rubric of 'blended worship', but only those with musical and spiritual ageusia savour the outcome. It seems more likely that Istanbul will again be called Constantinople than that the worship of Western Christianity will gather into one the dispersed children of the Reformation.

It is above this demented cacophony that Wright, Waltke, and others seek to make their voices heard. And if they are

17 Flynn, 'Liturgical Music', 771.

18 MacCulloch, *History of Christianity*, 486.

to make any difference, such voices must be heard above and outside stale debates about Psalms, hymns, and music. Those debates presuppose that the outline of worship with which we are familiar in Western Protestantism is not open to question: singing and music are an element of worship, which should last for the duration of four traditional hymns, or forty minutes, or until those with varicose veins need to sit down. The only question is, what should we sing and in what style? *The Westminster Confession of Faith* may carry the germ of such a post-1453 Western consensus when it classes the 'singing of psalms with grace in the heart' as a part 'of the ordinary religious worship of God' (21.5), no less than the reading of Scripture, preaching, prayer, or the sacraments (21.3–5). But, if the Westminster divines thought of singing Psalms as a distinct part of worship, and even a Christian duty,[19] they surely thought it a less significant part than it has become. Almost a century before Westminster, *The First Book of Discipline* (1560) did not rank singing 'utterly necessarie,' but only 'profitable,' since 'in some kirks the Psalmes may conveniently be sung, in others perchance they cannot.'[20] The contemporaneous *Second Helevetic Confession* took the same line: 'singing in sacred assemblies ought to be moderated *where it is in use*,' and no one should condemn churches 'which have faithful prayer in good manner, without any singing' (23.4).

If Leishman was right, this was still 'the prevalent feeling of the time'[21] when the Westminster Assembly met. *The Directory of Publick Worship* is certainly muted about the place of singing, sounding rather like *The First Book of Discipline* when

19 'Of Singing of Psalms,' *The Directory for the Publick Worship of God.*

20 *The First Book of Discipline: With Introduction and Commentary by James K. Cameron* (Edinburgh: St Andrew Press, 1972), 180.

21 Thomas Leishman ed., *The Westminster Directory* (Edinburgh: William Blackwood & Sons, 1901), 147.

it anticipates one Psalm, or perhaps two 'if with conveniency it may be done.'[22] The *Westminster Confession* itself has far more to say about prayer as a part of religious worship, perhaps mirroring their sometimes one or two-hour-long public prayers. We cannot blame the Reformers or Puritans that today we pray less and sing more, or that we divide over what they did not even count 'utterly necessary.' They were relatively unenthusiastic about music and singing in church because they sought to preserve whatever truly catholic elements and attitudes they had inherited from a millennium and a half of Christian worship.

In this light, the place given to music today, not least its adoption as a 'ministry', is surely unprecedented. Even if, however, the instrumental and performance element were eliminated, leaving us with only a few debates about what acapella songs to sing, we would still not be on the same wavelength as earlier Christians. They appeared not to begin with the presupposition 'We must sing,' leading to the inevitable question, 'What shall we sing?' Singing was a part of their worship only as the most fitting mode for some more fundamental activity, not as an end in itself. The responsorial sung 'Hallelujah' or 'Amen' of the ancient church had the obvious liturgical purpose of expressing praise, or believing concurrence with what had gone before. And what was true of these one-word responses was also true of the more extended use of Psalms in the liturgy (whenever they became a feature of worship).[23] Even in what became their standard use as antiphons near the beginning of a service, Psalm 103 (104) or 146 (147) have a responsive role, answering the call to worship and expressing gladness as God gathers his scattered flock together in Zion. The axiom and question, 'We must sing; what shall

22 Ibid., 39.

23 For historical discussion see Farrow, *Psalm Verses*, 17–21.

we sing?' did not shape the content of worship. Rather, divine commands and invitations, accusations and promises, demanded a response from Christian worshippers, and if they gave voice to that response, what would they say? 'Hallelujah'? 'Amen'? 'His mercy endures for ever'? Perhaps. But if that is not enough, if the church must put a more elaborate response into their mouths, whose words will provide a universal expression of the praise and thanks, hopes and fears, of the whole number of the elect?

For this, the church turned to the words of archetypal believers, which are recorded in Scripture, giving many Psalms a fixed place in the liturgy and the whole Psalter a daily role in Christian worship. Whether they were spoken, chanted, or sung was less important than that they provided fitting responses for yet-sinful worshippers in the company of heaven. And in providing those responses, they also impressed Scripture upon Christian hearts in a pre-print age, becoming the part or element of worship that the Reformers and Puritans wished to maintain in sung form, and the 'spiritual root system' for Christianity that Wright wants to restore. That will not happen, however, in the Western church or its international diaspora until it works out how to unwind several centuries of thinking, disentangling musical development from Christian worship, separating the concert hall from the sanctuary, and returning to a more fundamental axiom and question: 'We must respond to God; what shall we say?'

Enforced Conversion

The second development standing in the way of Wright and Waltke's reformation is theological. This is not to suggest that musical developments were theologically neutral, but that something primarily theological led to the 'great impoverishment'. That this deprivation came upon Western Christians and their forbears simultaneously with the surge of hymnody that began in the eighteenth-century may not be coincidental. Indeed, the real deprivation is not the replacement of Psalms with hymns, but the embrace of an approach to the Psalms that snatched them from Christian hands and buried them in the Ancient Near East.

It may not have been his aim, but Isaac Watts had a leading role in this process. Eighteenth-century psalmody was 'the great Occasion' of an 'Evil' as the 'Matter and Words' instead of elevating 'us to the most delightful and divine Sensations, doth not only flat our Devotion, but too often awakens our Regret, and touches all the Springs of Uneasiness within us.'[24] What was to be done with a part of the Old Testament that had 'a thousand Lines in it which were not made for a Church in our Days'?[25] Dissatisfied with previous Psalters that 'only make David *speak* English,'[26] Watts wanted '*David* converted into a Christian,'[27] offering the church an opportunity to purify her 'extreamly *Jewish* and cloudy'[28] Old Testament songs 'with the spirit of the Independent meeting house'[29] in *The Psalms of David Imitated* (1719). Were David able to see the result, he might wonder if Watts had done him more harm than Saul and Shimei combined.

But David has had to contend with more than enforced conversion. As a joint-victim of many Christian assaults upon

24 Isaac Watts, 'Preface' to *Hymns and Spiritual Songs* in Selma L. Bishop, *Isaac Watts Hymns and Spiritual Songs 1707–1748: A Study in Early Eighteenth Century Language Changes* (London: The Faith Press, 1962), li.

25 Ibid., lii.

26 Harry Escott, *Isaac Watts—Hymnographer: A Study of the Beginnings, Development, and Philosophy of the English Hymn* (London: Independent Press Ltd, 1962), 143.

27 Watts, *Hymns and Spiritual Songs*, lv.

28 Ibid, li.

29 Escott, *Watts*, 154.

the Old Testament, the psalmist has often been silenced. In the same century that Watts died, what became known as 'biblical theology' was born, and in churches that adopted Watts' legacy, perhaps biblical theology did more to formalize his attitude to the Old Testament than did his hymns. His de-historicizing and evangelizing of the Psalms might be anathema to most careful interpreters of the Old Testament. Many (especially the Welsh) would not agree that 'Judah and Israel may be called England and Scotland, and the Land of Canaan may be translated into Great Britain.'[30] That, however, does not mean that careful interpreters do not share his tendency to see a spiritual gulf between Jerusalem and Sydney, or Zion and Chicago, which means the Old Testament is best visited as a museum artefact—on-site and in its original setting. Whatever should happen to the Elgin Marbles, the Psalms should certainly be returned to Israel.

It might seem unfair to blame all this on biblical theology, which, after all, often aspires to trace the biblical plot line from creation to new creation. No doubt many cultural, philosophical, and theological trends have influenced the Western church's approach to the Old Testament during the last three centuries, but the methodology of biblical theology has established itself as the preeminent approach among conservative Protestants who espouse 'responsible' exegesis. Having attempted to describe biblical theology elsewhere,[31] I shall merely restate that Stendhahl's emphasis on the 'distinction between what it meant and what it means'[32] generally uncovers the face of

30 Isaac Watts, 'A Short Essay Toward the Improvement of Psalmody' in *The Works of the Reverend and Learned Isaac Watts, Vol. 4* (London: J. Barfield, 1810), 376.

31 Philip S. Ross, *From the Finger of God* (Fearn: Mentor: 2011), 41–50.

32 Krister Stendahl, 'Biblical Theology' in George Arthur Buttrick, ed., *The Interpreter's Dictionary of the Bible* (New York: Abingdon Press, 1962), 420.

biblical theology in the church. Any approach to the Old Testament, constrained by a notion of 'what it meant' within its historical context, and which limits meaning to that historical context, is bound to diminish its relevance to the church. 'What it meant' is in any case a slippery ideal even according to the Old Testament. What, for example, did Isaiah mean? And to whom? Someone may say, 'To his original audience.' But Isaiah could reply, 'They had no idea what I meant' (Isa 6:9–10). 'Well, in that case,' someone else may say, 'what he meant to himself—his intended meaning.' But did he know what he meant? We might suppose so, but prophets themselves sometimes 'heard' yet 'did not understand' (Dan. 12:8), or had to live by faith with an incomplete understanding of their own meaning (Hab. 2:3). According to the New Testament, such lack of understanding was not just about 'times and seasons' as in Acts 1:7, but about the essential meaning of the Old Testament (1 Pet. 1:10–11). Isaiah and his fellow prophets were guardians and proclaimers of a mystery, the meaning of which would not be revealed until God rent the heavens and came down in Jesus Christ (1 Cor. 2:7–9; Isa. 64:1–4). Even then, this meaning could only be revealed 'through the Spirit' (1 Cor. 2:10). Isaiah might still say to the careful, 'scientific' exegete, 'You have no idea what I meant.'

Applied to the Psalms, biblical theology, with the quiet assistance of some historical-critical presuppositions, produces results that will never restore the Psalter to its place as the 'spiritual root system' of Christianity. When the psalms are abandoned to some imagined historical ritual or setting, at best these roots become like coal, mined from biblical history to warm Christians with themes of praise and providence. They have nothing to say about the resurrection of the dead or the new creation, and little more to say about Jesus Christ humiliated and exalted. In which case, why would any Christian want to sing them, or even read them?

Fines & Penalties

The answer to this lies neither in the aggressive Christianizing of Watts, nor in unfettered Christocentric spiritualizing or allegorizing, but in an approach that is true to Scripture's interpretation of itself and which is willing to think that biblical authors may not have abused other parts of Scripture. If, for example, modern scholarship judges Hosea 11:1 to have meant something other than what Matthew seemed to think it meant (Matt. 2:15), can we not at least allow for the possibility that Matthew was right and scholarship is wrong? Are we bound to think that we can only read forwards from the Old Testament until progressive revelation either peters out in deep intertestamental darkness, or, in the case of a few gloriously explicit prophecies, bursts into great Gospel light?

Richard Hays, tackling the 'unconscious Marcionite bias… of many Protestant churches,'[33] argues for reading not just forwards, but also backwards because that is what Old and New Testaments teach us to do.[34] This does not mean denying or negating the Old Testament's literal or historical sense, but recognising that 'it becomes the vehicle for latent figural meanings unsuspected by the original author and readers.'[35] Perhaps some original authors and readers were more suspicious than Hays suspects, but recognising that according to the Gospels, 'those who fail to read the OT this way have not yet fully understood it'[36] may be a step towards a more biblical perspective. This applies equally to the Psalms as part of the Old Testament, although they may already be the focus of more calls for restoration to a living canon of Scripture. If

33 Richard B. Hays, *Reading Backwards: Figural Christology and the Fourfold Gospel Witness* (London: SPCK, 2015), 5.

34 Ibid., 4.

35 Ibid., 15.

36 Ibid., 16.

'for much of the church today, Moses and the prophets belong to a closed and unknown book,'[37] at least the Psalms still get to stand-in for them all in a hotel Bible.

Few calls to restore the Psalter leave the author facing a fine, but that is what happened to one twentieth-century author living under a government that had a particular antipathy to the Old Testament. Only after seeking to persuade the Reich Board for the Regulation of Literature that his work was 'scientific exegesis,' did Dietrich Bonhoeffer escape having to pay thirty Reichsmarks for publishing *The Prayerbook of the Bible: An Introduction to the Psalms.*[38] The Board might not have been unreasonable to judge his approach more theological than scientific. For Bonhoeffer, the Psalms are all about Jesus Christ, but not in the most obvious way. He reasons that we can only speak to God in the 'pure language that God has spoken to us in Jesus Christ,' language that Scripture teaches us, especially through the Psalms as the Bible's prayer book. It does not matter if the Psalms do not express our feelings—'we must pray against our own heart in order to pray rightly,' and in so doing we pray the Psalter simultaneously with Jesus Christ.[39] How is this possible?

> It is the incarnate Son of God, who has borne all human weakness in his own flesh, who here pours out the heart of all humanity before God, who stands in our place and prays for us. He has known torment and pain, guilt and death more deeply than we have. Therefore it is the prayer of the human nature assumed by Christ that comes before God here. It is really our prayer. But since the Son of God knows us better than we know ourselves, and was

37 Ibid.

38 Geffrey B. Kelley, 'Editor's Introduction to the English Edition' in *Dietrich Bonhoeffer Works, Vol.* 5 (Minneapolis: Fortress Press, 1996), 143.

39 *Dietrich Bonhoeffer,* 'Prayerbook of the Bible,' ibid., 156–7, 159.

> truly human for our sake, it is also really the Son's prayer. It can become our prayer only because it was his prayer.[40]

Bonhoeffer's approach has similar features to those Rowan Williams detects in Augustine, for whom 'the Psalms are the words of Jesus, the Word who speaks in all scripture.' We read the Psalms 'as spoken by the whole Christ, that is Christ with members of his Body,'[41] and in the 'church's worship…the singing of the psalms becomes the most immediate routine means of identifying with the voice of Christ.'[42] Whether or not Bonhoeffer could claim Augustine's legacy, that some North American evangelicals are as eager to claim Bonhoeffer as liberals are to retain him shows that the German's legacy is as controversial as his thought is unravellable. However one wishes to affirm or to critique his theology or Christology, his book does not reveal a comprehensible exegetical foundation for his approach to the Psalms. Yet he does express a common Christian instinct that, whatever scholarship may say, the first question we want to ask is not what the Psalms 'have to do with us, but what they have to do with Jesus Christ.'[43]

Fines are not the only potential peril facing those who wish to write on the Psalms. Douglas Green, a former teacher at Westminster Theological Seminary, did not come into conflict with the Reich Board, but his view of Psalm 23 played some role in his 'honorable retirement'[44] and the controversy that followed.[45] Green's essay is relevant to this discussion, being

40 Ibid., 159–60.

41 Rowan Williams, 'Augustine and the Psalms', *Interpretation*, January (2004), 21.

42 Ibid., 22.

43 Bonhoeffer, 'Prayerbook,' 157.

44 http://www.wts.edu/stayinformed/view.html?id=1794, accessed 5 Jan. 2016.

45 http://wrfnet.org/articles/2014/09/statement-support-dr-doug-green, accessed 5 January 2016.

'an attempt to "see Jesus" in Psalm 23 in a fresh way.'[46] He notes that Christians have long understood Psalm 23 to mean 'Jesus is my shepherd'.[47] From Augustine to Boice, interpreters have applied Psalm 23 to 'Christ's relationship with individual Christians.'[48] Augustine, however, might be best excluded since his opening statement—'The Church speaks to Christ'—suggests he did not read Psalm 23 so individualistically, but more as a corporate response to 'the person of The Crucified' who he identifies as the speaker in Psalm 22. In any case, Green concludes that the Jesus-is-my-shepherd approach to Psalm 23 testifies to a tension in how modern evangelicals interpret the Psalter: 'grammatical-historical interpretation means that the primary question we ask is, more or less, what did the psalm mean to its original author? With this hermeneutical tether in place, it is arguable that no psalms prophesy some distant messianic future because every psalm addresses the "here and now" of ancient Israel.'[49]

Green's solution lies in looking at the Psalter in its 'final form' and seeing that Psalms which did not 'have an eschatological orientation *at the level of their original composition* may be open to an eschatological or prophetic reinterpretation in their new literary context'.[50] In other words, Psalm 18 or Psalm 127 may originally only have been concerned with the 'here and now' of their author's day, but when the 150 Psalms were gathered into one Psalter they became potentially concerned with the elsewhere and yet-to-be. This may prove hugely confusing to

46 Douglas J. Green, '"The LORD Is Christ's Shepherd": Psalm 23 as Messianic Prophecy' in *Eyes to See, Ears to Hear: Essays in Memory of J. Alan Groves*, eds. Peter Enns, Douglas J. Green, & Michael B. Kelly (Phillipsburg: P&R Publishing, 2010), 33.

47 Ibid., 34.

48 Ibid., 34–5.

49 Ibid., 35.

50 Ibid., 36.

the Christian who trusts his Bible and wants to know what the Psalms 'have to do with Jesus Christ.' If a Psalm is only prophetic when it finally takes its place as Psalm 40 or Psalm 102, who was the inspired author? The psalmist? Some unknown layout editor, following whose inspiration they acquire a status akin to Paul's citation of a pagan poet (Acts 17:28)? Both psalmist and editor? Who knows? Should Jesus and his apostles have been a little more tentative about the Psalms' authorship and authorial intent?

There is certainly no doubt for Green that Jesus and the New Testament authors understood the Psalms as prophecies fulfilled in Christ.[51] And he has no wish to reject their readings, but to multiply them, so that we 'read the *whole* of the Psalter in a prophetic and eschatological direction...as messianic psalms that describe the different dimensions of the life—and especially the suffering—of Israel's eschatological King.'[52] The example he offers in Psalm 23 is a 'second type of Christological reading', standing alongside, but not replacing what he calls 'the traditional Christian interpretation that places Jesus in the role of Yahweh.' Second time round, Jesus is the sheep and the Father is his Shepherd.[53]

It is not necessary to discuss the conclusions of Green's exposition, which may not be so novel, either exegetically or theologically; the question is not so much about the destination as the route. Is Green right that 'Christian interpretation of the OT must be an exercise in reading backwards, of rereading earlier texts so that their meanings cohere with what God has actually done in history in Jesus Christ'?[54] Surely—such rereading is inescapable. But if that rereading implies the

51 Ibid., 37.

52 Ibid., 37–8.

53 Ibid., 38.

54 Ibid., 43.

imposition of a different meaning to that of the original author, whether he understood it clearly or proclaimed it as a mystery, it is less satisfactory. If, on the other hand, the rereading uncovers a fuller meaning, which divine judgment veiled to previous readers, or which could not be grasped by an inspired prophet until the fullness of the time had come, then that is a different matter.

But sheep or Shepherd, could the conclusions flowing from Green's placement of Jesus Christ in Psalm 23 not emerge from rereading that is more sympathetic to the Old Testament text?

Christocentric Continuity

The idea that any biblical interpreter can read the Old Testament in an intellectually-pristine, historically-contained environment, unaffected by the theology of the New Testament and dogmatic presuppositions, so that he or she arrives at a meaning perfectly replicating what was in the author's mind, is so absurd that it merits no refutation. Even Judaism interprets the Old Testament in a way that is influenced by its knowledge of what it rejects in the New. This does not mean, however, that the inevitability of reading backwards should eliminate every attempt to read forwards, nor should it lead to a kind of hopeless Christological interpretation, which sees Christ in all the Scriptures only because he said as much. If his lecture on the move was an exercise in hermeneutics (Luke 24:27), we should perhaps judge it difficult rather than hopeless.

When it comes to the Psalms, some may argue, as Green pointed out, that 'no psalms prophesy some distant messianic future.' Others, still wishing to claim loyalty to the original meaning, may decide that only certain Psalms are messianic, however they may define 'messianic'. Beyond that, and general themes of fulfilment, there may seem little scope for Christological interpretation without resort to theological imposition or reading backwards against the grain. John Calvin's solution in one case (Hebrews' use of Psalm 8) was to answer the argument that the Psalm is not 'speaking of one man, but of all mankind' with the claim that 'this is no reason why these words should not be applied to the person of Christ.'[55] That, however, is only to describe the New Testament authors' unsympathetic rereading euphemistically. It is liable to Owen's accusation that when 'some would have the literal sense to respect mankind in general, and what is affirmed in them to be mystically applied unto Christ,' then 'the words have no sense at all.'[56] But perhaps there are ways of reading all Psalms forwards, which pay attention to non-speculative details of original authorship and context, and which also move in a continuous trajectory towards the New Testament. In that case, reading backwards will not establish a 'reinterpretation' or 'double sense' but only allow us to see the route from first light to perfect day, and from apprehension to comprehension—insofar as such fullness is possible in this age.

Beginning with the 'hymnwriting workshops'[57] of King David in 1 Chronicles 25, Michael Lefebvre sets out what may be a first step in reading all the Psalms forwards. He seeks to establish that 'in biblical worship, it is the king who leads the congregation into worship, and it is the king's own songs that the congregation sings with him.'[58] This principle, enshrined in the hymn collections of the First Temple, is preserved in the five books of the 150 Psalms that Ezra compiled—'remarkable…in a hymnal compiled in an era when there was no longer a king

55 John Calvin, *The Epistle of Paul the Apostle to the Hebrews*, trans. Willaim B. Johnston (Grand Rapids: Eerdmans, 1994), 21.

56 John Owen, *An Exposition of the Epistle to the Hebrews, Vol. 3* (Edinburgh: Banner of Truth, 1991), 363.

57 Michael Lefebvre, *Singing the Songs of Jesus: Revisiting the Psalms* (Fearn: Christian Focus Publications, 2010), 32.

58 Ibid., 43.

on Mount Zion.'[59] It also holds good for the New Testament church, which worships with Jesus, Son of David, as he takes the role of his forefather. This is not a reinterpretation of the Psalter: 'David wrote with awareness of the coming Son of David who would ultimately take the Psalms to his lips as our perfect king and songleader.'[60] We will return to these themes when we come to the text of Psalms 113–118, but such an approach opens the way for an interpretation of the Psalms marked by Christocentric continuity from the point of authorship to fulfilment. Applied to Psalm 23, an interpreter's conclusions may bear similarities to Green's, but the exegetical direction yields to the flow of biblical revelation rather than creating a whirlpool.

The argument that the worship-leading of Israel's king reaches its enduring highpoint in the Christ might be less significant were it not for the New Testament's apparent adoption of the theme. Beyond passages such as Mark 12:35–37, Lefebvre mentions Hebrews 2,[61] and it is common to assert that Christ's quotation of Psalm 22 presents him as our worship leader (more of this in the Interlude). It is of even greater interest for this book that Psalm 117 may have a similar function in Romans 15, while in 2 Corinthians 4, Paul finds Psalm 116 a description of his own Christ-like sufferings. Matthew Scott has provided us with a study of those two passages where 'Christ might be installed as speaking subject, whether he is named for them or not.'[62] He focuses on *metalepsis,* which 'is

59 Michael Lefebvre, 'The Hymns of Christ: The Old Testament Formation of the New Testament Hymnal' in *Sing a New Song.* eds. Joel R. Beeke and Anthony T. Selvaggio (Grand Rapids: Reformation Heritage Books, 2010), Kindle Location 2166–89.

60 Lefebvre, *Singing the Songs of Jesus*, 53.

61 Ibid., 50–51.

62 Matthew Scott, *The Hermeneutics of Christological Psalmody in Paul: An Intertextual Enquiry* (New York: Cambridge University Press, 2014), 31.

conventionally taken to involve the metonymical substitution of one word by another which is itself a metonym.'[63] As if that were not complicated enough, he adds 'suture' to the mix, which turns out to be neither surgical nor anatomical, but a notion 'borrowed from the semiotics of film, and refers to a speaker's agreement to be represented by the subject of the cinematic text (the camera); in the case of a psalm, by the psalm's subject of speech.'[64] So in the case of Psalm 23, suture is about how the reader—you, me, Paul, Ezra, or Jesus—identifies with the psalmist who said, 'The LORD is my shepherd.' This matters when we come to cases like Paul's citations of Psalm 116 or Psalm 117. If, for Paul, these words are Christ's words, in what way does Christ identify with the psalmist? Does the whole Psalm speak of the Saviour's experience? It is not possible to discuss Scott's sophisticated contribution in detail, but the relevance of such questions to the idea that Christ is now the anointed king who leads our worship is obvious, and we will return to these matters when we come to those Psalms.

If the 'great impoverishment' that Wright lamented is to be reversed, perhaps it will only happen when the Western church builds on the observations of writers such as Lefebvre and Scott, developing an approach to the Psalter that recognises Christocentric continuity—not unsympathetic to the original context, yet willing to yield to the New Testament's evaluation of that context and its writers. Whether Christian churches sing, chant, or otherwise pray the Psalms, lively believers will only make them their 'spiritual root system' if they can see how the Psalms bring them to know Christ better, not just because he somehow fulfilled them, but because through them God poured grace upon Christ's lips and life, and through them the Spirit strengthened his faith.

63 Ibid., 4.

64 Ibid., 28, n. 104.

Sometimes history's great figures may appear to have been born too soon; they are more successful in death than in life. At the first performance of Beethoven's Third Symphony one listener shouted, 'I'll give another *Kreutzer* if the thing will only stop!' One year later, in 1806, when Beethoven launched his sixteen string quartets (Op. 59), belligerent performers vented their frustration. The cellist Berhard Romberg reacted so badly to an opening solo that 'he threw his music to the ground and stamped on it,' while 'violinist Felix Radicati was bold enough to describe the new quartets in the composer's presence as "not music". Beethoven retorted, "Oh, they are not for you, they are for a later age."'[65]

While some readers of the Psalms tend to say to themselves, 'They are not for me, they were for an earlier age,' Beethoven's retort gives a truer assessment: 'they are for a later age.' However ancient authors and singers may have appreciated the Psalms, only when they become the Saviour's songbook, and only as he leads the people of God in song, do they come of age. The Psalms were 'for a later age'—for the age of the Spirit-filled Christian, whose Christ-procured understanding grants him or her the privilege of singing these songs with 'open face'. This age is not the time to put away the Psalms as if we had exhausted their meaning. Much has yet to be fulfilled, and as with the song of Moses (Rev. 15:3), their best performance is yet to come. Written across every attempt to interpret the Psalms must be this disclaimer: 'Now I know in part.'

Two Distinct Natures—One Person Forever

The final matter to raise before turning to the Hallel is about Jesus Christ. Even if we concentrate on the text of the Psalms,

65 Edward Dusinberre, *Beethoven for a Later Age: The Journey of a String Quartet* (London: Faber & Faber, 2016), 98–9.

when we ask what it meant for Christ to sing those Psalms before he went to the Mount of Olives, we cannot answer that question without recourse to what we already believe about Jesus Christ. Those convictions cannot be determined by the text of Psalms 113–118, or even their New Testament citations in isolation, only by Scripture's overall witness and by the church's expression of that witness in her creeds and confessions. The Chalcedonian Creed of 451 AD still expresses what orthodox Christians believe about Jesus Christ, that he is one person in two natures, 'truly God and truly man'. The confessions of the Reformed churches echo that creed, and only with their understanding of his two natures can Jesus' use of the Psalms make sense. The man Christ Jesus did not know everything. When in perplexity he took the Psalms on his lips, he meant every word. How did he know what he knew about God?—'in the only way that such knowledge is possible for man: by revelation.'[66] When that revelation was the Scriptures, the Holy Spirit gave him an understanding of his Father and of himself that was in no way defective, yet truly human. He had to grow in every way (Luke 2:40).

When the time comes for him to sing Psalms 113–118 at Passover, our Spirit-taught Saviour is near the peak of his human knowledge in his state of humiliation, yet he will learn more about his Father and his will, about himself and his task, as he sings these psalms with his disciples. What that meant we can never know exhaustively, but we can recognise that before us we have six Psalms, which we do not understand at all if we understand them differently from Jesus. They confronted him with an approaching horror that would make him sweat blood, yet they also opened up to him the joy that was set before him, so that he endured the cross, despised the shame, and sits now at the right hand of God.

66 Donald MacLeod, *The Person of Christ* (Leicester: IVP, 1998), 166.

3

Praise the Lord!

Psalm 113

If you were Jean Rabec, the tongueless singer with which this book began, what Psalm would you have chosen? Perhaps he did not have to choose. Psalm 79 was standard martyrs' fare for the Huguenots, as it also was for Roman Catholics when Protestants trashed their monasteries, but we will keep quiet about that.

A little like Jean Rabec, Jesus did not have to choose a final Psalm. It was Passover, and Psalms 113–118 were the Psalms appointed for that day. To sing anything else would have been so odd it might merit a comment in the biblical record. But were these Psalms appropriate? Knowing what you know about Jesus Christ, about who he was and what he suffered, what Psalms would you have suggested he sing during the last twenty-four hours of his life? Would some other Psalm or Psalms have been more fitting than Psalms 113–118? What about Psalm 22? He would quote that later. Or Psalm 31? He would mention that too. Psalm 69? The waters would soon come up over his head. Psalm 23? Perhaps. But would the Lord be with him when he went through death's dark vale?

No doubt it would have been ungodly impertinence to tell Jesus what Scripture best fitted his needs. He knew and understood the Psalms better even than their authors. But more than that, it was not simply Jewish tradition that chose his final hymn; God did that for him. Just as his disciples would look back and see him nailed to the cross according to 'the determined purpose and foreknowledge of God' (Acts 2:23), that evening Jesus saw himself not as a tragic victim of traitorous brethren, but as following a path that God had determined (Luke 22:22). And would he not have seen that fatherly hand in every detail of his experience? Whatever historical circumstances brought Psalms 113–118 together, and however they came to be associated with Passover, it was a work of providence, the highest end of which may have been that these Psalms would minister to Jesus on the eve of his death. God made them an indispensable element in everything that came together to make Christ do what he came to do.

So now on the eve of his crucifixion, while Jesus remembers God's saving acts with his disciples, these six psalms enliven their fellowship as he offers himself to them, contemplates what he is about to suffer for them, and anticipates being in the Father's kingdom with them. Even as they sing, the Holy Spirit ministers to Jesus, strengthening his resolve and his faith. Through these songs, Jesus receives new insights into what he came to do, into what he is about to suffer, and into the glory to follow. And out of this spiritual bounty, Jesus ministers to his disciples. They do not understand what is happening. Shortly they will forsake him and flee. But as he sings with them, he plants a song in their hearts that will never fade. Soon, they will sing these Psalms as a new song to the LORD, with Spirit-filled understanding.

[1] Hallelujah!

Praise, O servants of the LORD!
Praise the name of the LORD.
[2] Blessed be the name of the LORD,
from now and forever.
[3] From the rising of the sun to its setting,
the name of the LORD is to be praised.

[4] The LORD is high (רום) above all nations,
his glory above the heavens.
[5] Who is like the LORD our God,
who dwells (ישׁב) on high,
[6] who humbles himself
to see things in heaven and earth?

[7] He raises the poor from the dust,
lifts (רום) the needy from the ash heap.
[8] To seat (ישׁב) them with princes,
with the princes of the people.
[9] He sets (ישׁב) the barren woman in a home—
a joyful mother of sons.

Hallelujah!

As the first psalm in the Hallel, Psalm 113 makes the opening call to united praise. It is also the Hallel's unifying theme, the alpha and omega of the psalm: 'Hallelujah'—'Praise the Lord' (vv. 1, 9). Perhaps, like me, you have been to some Christian gatherings where a preacher or worship leader tries to stir people up, saying things like, 'Praise the LORD! There's something in the air today, the Spirit is really moving in this place. Do you really, really, really want to praise the LORD?' Of course you do really, really, really want to praise the LORD, but his or her exertions are not helping in the slightest. You don't feel stirred up. You just think, 'Oh, give us a break.' Fair enough—that sort of whipping never made anyone praise the LORD. It's stupidity, verging on blasphemy.

But that is not what we find in Psalm 113. Repeated hallelujahs—yes, but they are not mindless. The psalmist does not stoop to legalistic hectoring. Between these opening and closing hallelujahs, he packs fuel for praise and truth to believe, which give this call to worship impulsive force. There are three components to this:

- A call to worship with the greatest congregation in the universe (vv. 1–3).
- An ultimate question: 'Who is like the LORD?' (vv. 4–6).
- The LORD exalts his servants (vv. 7–9).

A Call to Worship

Psalm 113's call to worship is not universal. It goes out not to the whole earth, but to people gathered out of the world into the service of God: 'Praise, O servants of the LORD' (v. 1).

Who are these servants? Are they the temple priests of Psalm 134 and 135, or are they men like Moses, Joshua, and David, who had to lead God's people in worship? Although such people were 'servants of the LORD', every Israelite was called to 'serve the LORD' (Deut. 10:12) and there is no reason to think this exhortation—'Praise, you servants of the LORD'—was only for choir and clergy. It comes to everyone who seeks to serve him. The best identity check for the 'servants of the LORD' is not the question, 'Are they priests, prophets, or kings?' but, 'What is their attitude?' Whoever walks in his ways and keeps his commandments, loving, seeking, and serving him with all their heart and soul is 'a servant of the LORD,' and a worshipper in this congregation.

When the psalmist goes on to say, 'Praise the name of the LORD' (v. 1b), 'Blessed be the name of the LORD' (v. 2) perhaps he appears repetitive, as if just saying the same thing in different words. Could he not just say, 'Hallelujah,' and leave us to get on with it? That might be fine if this were a call to imaginative engagement with an unknown God, but this God has a name—a name that proclaims his character and defines how we must engage with him.

This earth's creator, Adam's father, Jacob's saviour, this merciful God, Israel's keeper, Judah's ruler, gracious giver of the law, slow-to-anger steadfast lover, faithful guardian to the thousandth generation, this relentless prosecutor of guilty fathers and unrepentant children, unblinded judge, great king of all the earth—the LORD is his name. He is who he is. What he is, is what he has been. What he will be, is what he is now. From everlasting to everlasting, the God of Jacob changes not.

And it's all in his name. Praise his name, and we praise him for all that he is, all that he has been, and all that he will be. Bless his name, and we go a step further; we approve, own, and embrace all that he is and does. We do not come to the Old Testament, read of what the LORD has done, and say, 'We don't approve of that.' Nor do we turn to the New Testament, and read of Christ's sacrificial death, or his coming judgment, and say, 'We can't endorse that.' Neither manufactured joy, nor contrived solemnity will be the wellspring of our praise and blessing, but rather an unreserved espousal of this God, whose name is 'the LORD'.

So we think of his mercy and grace, from Eden to Egypt, from first Passover to final sacrifice, we see how patiently he dealt with Jacob's sons, how he would not forsake his covenant, and we gladly acknowledge that his love to whoring Israel was a love for the whole world that would yet bring many sons and daughters into his banqueting house. No broken old covenant could hold back love so steadfast. No empty throne could confine faithfulness so devoted to one generation. His love still lays hold of the needy and makes their families like flocks, not forsaking children and children's children, but preserving them and disciplining them as sons. This is how our God deals with us; praise the name of the LORD.

But what if, though standing in this great congregation, I fear that he should pass me by? After all, he will by no means clear the guilty, and I am guilty. If my sins and faults of youth still scar my memory, will he forget them? When iniquities prevail against me, when besetting sins defeat me, will he atone for my transgressions? If there is some limit to his charity, have I not reached it? Surely he would be just in judging me and in doing nothing to hold back the visitation of my iniquities upon my children. How I fear him.

If I fear him like that, do I not also bless his name? I would not find him praiseworthy and perfect if he cleared the guilty. With the whole congregation, I bless his name that he will deal with all the injustice and evil of this weary world, that evildoers great and small, who slipped away peacefully, unrepentant and unpunished, will not evade his justice. So what is there for me to do, but entrust myself to him, even to his uncompromising justice, persuaded that he will reconcile me to himself in a way that is wholly consistent with his holy character? Days may still come when I say, 'I don't understand. The LORD's ways are a mystery to me.' But all true worshippers in this congregation go on to say, 'Yet I believe, I praise the name of the LORD, I bless his holy name, so that one day I will understand.' As we focus upon the LORD, like the psalmist in these first three Psalms (113–115), we are not preoccupied with ourselves, but so taken up with the LORD's goodness to his people that we can only say, 'Blessed be the name of the LORD.'

If this is the greatest congregation in the universe, what makes it so? The first part of the answer comes in the words following that exhortation in verse 2: 'from now and forevermore.' To hear the call to 'Praise the LORD' and join this congregation, praising and blessing his name, is to enter into an experience that will last forever. This is not a service that will end with a benediction. Nor is it a collage of momentary thrills and temporary joys gathered from high holy days. To worship with this congregation is to put yourself in the flow of a blessing that will never cease. Just to be part of it is about the greatest privilege one could ever have. Israelites could sing this psalm at Passover, thinking of the Exodus from Egypt, but if they had any spiritual insight, they knew that was only the beginning, and that they would again, 'see the salvation of the LORD,' and somehow praise him for it in a congregation that would span every generation.

The second part of the answer comes in verse 3: 'From the rising of the sun to its setting, the name of the LORD is to be praised.' It's going to be big. Jerusalem will be too small. Judah will not hold it. From where the sun rises to where it sets, in every nation under the sun, in every tribe and tongue, the name of the LORD is to be praised. Someday the praises of the LORD's servants will break all territorial boundaries, and this congregation will not only span generations, but cross nations.

When would the great congregation of this Psalm become a reality? What might our Lord Jesus have thought about that as he sang Psalm 113 with his disciples in the Upper Room? As a true and a real man, Jesus did not know everything. All that he knew and believed about himself, he learned from the Scriptures and by God's Holy Spirit. So what does he think as he sings these words? How big does he suppose this congregation will be? We need not speculate. Jesus has already answered that: 'People,' he said, 'will come from east and west, and from north and south, and sit down in the kingdom of God' (Luke 13:29). He sings these words with them now, knowing that through what he is about to suffer, he will prepare a place for them, and countless others, so that his house will be filled.

As worshippers in that great congregation, we praise the LORD, not only with his servants across the nations, and not only with the different generations that make up God's people, but with a great company 'who rejoice with us, but upon another shore and in a greater light.' And who speaks to us now in this Psalm? Is it only an unnamed, ancient psalmist who calls on us to 'Praise the Lord'? Twenty centuries ago, our Lord Jesus sang these words with his disciples at the Passover table. He sang not just as a child of Abraham, but as a son of David—the offspring of a royal line, whose task it was to call God's people to worship and to lead them into the presence of God. This is still his song. He sings, not now at the Passover table, but with the whole company of heaven, leading his congregation in everlasting praise. Jesus Christ calls us to worship. Saints above join him and call us to worship. Saints on earth, joining them, call us to worship—some newborn into the kingdom, some suffering for Christ, some about to pass into glory—yet all say with one voice: 'Praise the name of the LORD. Blessed be the name of the LORD, from this time forth and forevermore.'

Who Is Like the Lord?

The congregation has a question: 'Who is like the LORD our God?' (v. 5). It seems to be an easy question with an obvious answer. We could simply say, 'No one. Absolutely no one,' and leave it at that. But should we? Is it little more than a rhetorical question that needs no second thought? The answer 'No one' is certainly not obvious to everyone. In any case, although that brief question captures the message of verses 4–6, the psalmist's question is somewhat more extended. The truncated question—'Who is like the LORD?'—may well be unanswerable, but there is no point in trying to answer that question without first asking, '*What* is the LORD like?' The psalm does tell us this much: The LORD is high—exalted—raised above all nations, and his glory above the heavens (v. 4).

That is an answer. But what does it mean? We could translate it into theological language and say, God is 'infinite, eternal, and unchangeable.' But what does that mean? Does anyone know? Perhaps the adjectives are the problem and we need to take Mark Twain's advice: 'When you catch an adjective, kill it.' If we could instead *show* what God is like so that the feelings those adjectives are meant to invoke spring from our hearts, then we would know what God is like. No doubt there is some truth in that. 'In the beginning God' shows us something that 'eternal' cannot tell us. 'In the beginning God created' displays what 'omnipotent' cannot convey. But still, 'What is the LORD like?'

The problem of answering goes beyond a choice between adjectives or nouns and verbs. To comprehend what it means for God to be infinite, I would need to be infinite. To fully understand what it means for God to be eternal, I would need to be eternal. We barely have the slightest understanding:

> All the rational conceptions of the minds of men are swallowed up and lost, when they would exercise themselves directly on that which is absolutely immense, eternal, infinite. When we say it is so, we know not what we say, but only that it is not otherwise. What we deny of God, we know in some measure—but what we affirm we know not; only we declare what we believe and adore.[1]

1 John Owen, *The Person of Christ* (Fearn: Christian Heritage, 2015), 114.

Indeed. The best that we can do is say what these things do not mean, or explain them by what God is not. He is infinite—never anxious about an uncertain future nor straining after greater knowledge of a mysterious universe, never conscious of weakness nor yearning for increased vitality, never a touch morose nor moderately joyful. He is eternal—he inhabits a dimension undiscoverable and unexplored, outside every beginning and ending. Our thoughts about God are inadequate. We speak true words, but no human vocabulary can chart the limits of his being.

That is what the psalmist wants to convey in verse 4. The LORD is beyond us—above the nations, above the heavens, altogether distinct and separate from his creation. We look up into the heavens and see in the night sky a picture worth… how many words? Who can say? Even all the galaxies and constellations combined would stammer and stutter if they tried to declare the essential glory of his being. No sight nor sound can capture his holy majesty. No words, no pictures, no music. Nothing. 'Holy, holy, holy, is the LORD…' Who is like the LORD our God?

Yet despite all this, the LORD is not anonymous power. The first indication of that comes in verse 5: the LORD dwells, sits, is enthroned, on high. Yes, the LORD is remote, above the nations, but if he is enthroned, then he is a king; he reigns, and somehow relates to his creatures. And perhaps the psalmist hints at something more homely. The LORD is certainly enthroned, but this king's palace is not an echoey, utilitarian monstrosity. It's a home, a family home, a place of joy and gladness, love and security, fit for a perfect royal family. We will return to that idea in verses 8–9, but for now we think of the LORD high above all, content and happy in himself, dwelling in unimaginable beauty and brilliance.

Why would he change that? Why would God distance himself from the realms of glory? It makes no sense to suppose that he would. But he does. 'He humbles himself—stoops down to look on the heavens and the earth' (v. 6). How strange! Surely he has no need to advance his knowledge. He is not like a king in his palace, who must dress as a tramp and spend a night under a railway bridge to understand the real world. The LORD already knows all things. Nor is this just a way of saying that he looks down on earth from afar, and asks, 'What is going on down there?' He is not scanning some unreachable spot from a celestial observatory, like the divine inverse of an astronomer. He 'humbles' himself. He makes himself low. Coming after verses 4–5, this does not seem a very god-like way to behave. God should not do this to himself; this is how he should treat the wicked, as in Psalm 147:6 where he casts the wicked to the ground and makes them low—empties them.

Why does a God so high, so separate, do this to himself? He humbles himself 'to see'—not in the sense of coming to take a look, nor out of curiosity, but to provide. This sounds like Abraham's God. If you met him somewhere, you would call the place Jehovah Jireh, 'the LORD will see,' 'the LORD will provide' (Gen. 22:14). Even so, how does this make sense—a God so high, humbling himself to somehow provide for his creation. 'Who is like the LORD our God?'

The psalmist's question 'recalls Exodus 15:11, "Who is like unto thee, O LORD among the gods?"' and 'the act for which God was shown to be incomparable...the Exodus.'[2] But if a 'parallel is intended,' is the parallel only between the exodus from Egypt and the exodus from Babylonian exile?[3] However wonderful the deliverance from Babylon, it was not in the same earth-shaking category as the Exodus. Cyrus and Artaxerxes were no Pharaohs. Anyone who thought the return from exile was equal to the Exodus had a smaller God than Moses. If a

2 Goulder, *Psalms of the Return*, 161.

3 Ibid.

parallel is intended with Exodus 15, it can only be to a work of greater significance, which will make God's people ask with fresh astonishment, 'Who is like the LORD our God?'

What must it have been like for our Saviour to sing this with his disciples on the eve of his crucifixion? He praises the name of the LORD. His view of the glory and splendour of God is clearer than that of any man. Yet he must weigh up this question: 'Who is like the LORD our God?' What must Jesus say to this? After all, he is the man who made so many claims to be this God. He had just said to his disciples, 'You believe in God, believe also in me' (John 14:1).

Who is like the LORD our God? It's the man at the table, singing Psalm 113. That's why he's at the table—because the LORD humbles himself, empties himself, to see, to provide for all those who eat and drink with him. This 'self-emptying' is the kind of divine act of which Psalm 113 speaks,[4] yet no one meditating on the psalmist's words could have predicted this: 'it was an inconceivable condescension and abasement, not only to behold, but take upon him (into personal union) our nature with himself.'[5] Only now, at the table with Jesus, has the psalmist's question found its intended parallel—not a parallel of precise equivalence and equality in God's act of deliverance, but a parallel in that the exodus and the incarnation were both wholly unparalleled acts of this incomparable God, who makes himself low.

How low? How low will he go? Lower. Much lower yet. Jesus will sing about that in the Psalms that follow, but for now, he goes forward to die in faith, believing that in what he is about to do, the whole universe will find an answer to this question: Who is like the LORD our God?

4 John Owen, *The Glory of Christ* (Fearn, Christian Heritage, 2004), 93.

5 John Owen, *Communion with God* (Fearn, Christian Heritage, 2007), 215

The Lord Exalts His Servants

Why does the LORD make himself low? Verses 7–9 give the answer. He does it 'to raise the poor from the dust, and to lift the needy from the ash heap.' This poor man or woman, is not in the kind of poverty that means they lack certain things, but somehow survive. This is destitution—someone so weak and helpless that unless help comes, they will be trampled into the dust. It is the poverty you feel when you come before the majesty of the LORD our God who dwells on high. It is the impotence you feel in the face of death, when we see written across our existence, 'Dust you are, and to dust you will return' (Gen. 3:19), and when we hear a voice calling in our direction, 'Return, O son of man.' And there is nothing you can do. Indeed, the situation is even worse. Before the face of God, I find myself not just poor, not only in the dust, but so needy that I am on the ash heap. In the light of his presence, all that I am is exposed—my sin, my shameful deeds, my sordid history and self-pitying discontent. I am disgraced. And in my disgrace, I am too ashamed to be anywhere other than where refuse belongs—on the dunghill and on the ash heap.

That is where I would stay, where all convicted sinners would stay, were it not for the LORD our God who humbles himself. He does not but look down and say with pitying eye, 'Oh, how I feel your pain.' He descends into the dust and onto the ash heap, to a place of contempt, outside the city. And this is no mere sympathetic gesture or act intended to add credibility to kind words. He raises, he lifts, he seats them with princes.

Recognise the language? The psalmist uses the vocabulary of verses 4–5. He wants us to know that when God lifts the needy, he bridges the unbridgeable, and *raises* them to be with himself, *raised* above the nations. Just as the LORD dwells on high, or *sits* enthroned, they too will *sit* with princes and dwell in the palace of the king, not as guests, but as children. This is how the LORD establishes his perfect royal family. No shame or disgrace now, no poverty or need; the LORD has raised them up. They have dignity beyond imagination. They reign with him forever and ever.

As our Lord Jesus sang these words, he knew that it was his task to bring about this great reversal for the poor and needy. How low he had already come. From the glory he had with the Father before the world began, down into a broken world. And he will go down, down, down—down lower than sin's consequences could take the greatest sinner. But Jesus believes what he sings. He believes that even if he should descend into Hell, his God will raise him to the highest place, and glorify him again, with the glory he had with him before the world began. He was with God in the beginning, dwelling on high, and tomorrow he will be back home in his Father's house, bringing with him a number that no man can number.

Some of the most ancient expositors thought that is what this last verse is about: 'He gives the barren woman a home, making her the joyous mother of children' (v. 9).[6] Regardless of the complications involved in interpreting this theme, particularly as it relates to Galatians 4:21–31, it would be strange if this were an unrelated appendage concerning female infertility, which had no connection with what has gone before. She knows the poverty of the ash heap too, not so much in her inability to sustain life as in her inability to create it. But the LORD will not neglect her. Her deliverance is directly equivalent to being seated with princes. Verses 8 and 9 use the same verb to describe the resettlement of the poor and needy.

6 Augustine of Hippo, *Expositions of the Psalms 99–120*, trans. Maria Boulding (New York: New City Press, 2003), 303. Theodoret of Cyrus, 'Commentary on Psalms 73–150' in *The Fathers of the Church*, Vol. 102, trans. Robert C. Hill (Washington DC: Catholic University of America Press), 222.

The LORD gathers them all together so that where he dwells they will dwell, where he *sits* they will *sit* also.

So who is the barren woman? And who are all her children? Verses 7–8 are almost a direct quotation from Hannah's song in 1 Samuel 2. Jesus' mother, Mary, echoed those words in her song, the Magnificat (Luke 1:46–55). Did Jesus think of her as he sang verse 9? Like Hannah, she wanted to proclaim that God had done for her something beyond explanation, taking her from obscurity and giving her a home. If the future of God's people often depended on a woman with a barren womb giving birth, ultimately their salvation depended on a woman with a virgin womb giving birth to Emmanuel.

Psalm 113 could almost be a hymnodic précis of a large part of Isaiah's prophecy, from the divine grandeur of Isaiah 40, 'Behold your God', on to the humbled servant of Isaiah 53, stricken, smitten, and silent, bearing the sin of many, and then to the exaltation and exultation of Isaiah 54, 'Sing, O barren one…the children of the desolate one will be more than the children of her who is married.' However precisely we may judge those prophecies to be fulfilled in the gospel, we praise the name of the LORD now as worshippers in this great congregation, because the LORD who dwells on high humbled himself to see. He made himself low to raise the needy on high, and to make the desolate woman a mother of many children, filling the Jerusalem above.

So as we hear this call to praise the LORD, as we take our places in the great congregation, as we ask, 'Who is like the LORD our God?' as we see our LORD Jesus humbling himself, as we sing these words with him, and as he raises us up, there is only one thing to say, 'Hallelujah—Praise the Lord.'

4

Tremble, O Earth!

Psalm 114

What are we to make of Psalm 114? Surely if any Psalm was intended for hoary Jews, and not for today's church, this is it. How could this Psalm have afforded Jesus any new insight or comfort in his night of agony? It might seem obscure to us today, but not so long ago Psalm 114 was moderately famous. Several prominent composers, notably Mendelssohn, produced significant choral works based on this Psalm. Perhaps that was because however obscure it may appear, the message of its anonymous author is always contemporary: 'Tremble, O earth at the presence of the LORD' (v. 7).

Psalm 113 called on the servants of the LORD, to praise the LORD as members of a great congregation, spanning every nation and generation, uniting heaven and earth in everlasting praise for the work of the God who humbles himself to raise us to the highest place. In Psalm 114, it is as if this great congregation turns to address the whole earth, and we say,

1 When Israel went out of Egypt,
the house of Jacob from people of strange speech.
2 Judah was his sanctuary
Israel his dominion.
3 The sea saw and fled,
Jordan turned back,
4 the mountains skipped like rams,
the hills like lambs.
5 What troubles you, O sea, that you flee,
O Jordan that you turn back
6 O mountains, that you skip like rams,
O hills, like lambs?

7 Tremble, O earth, at the presence of the LORD,
At the presence of the God of Jacob,
8 who turns the rock into a water pool,
the flint into a water spring.

'Listen, O earth, you disregard our God, you think nothing of him humbling himself to raise us up. Well, think again. Whoever you are, wherever you are, what our God has done will turn your life upside down. Accept him or reject him, honour him or despise him, sooner or later you must face the consequences of what God has done for us.'

Psalm 114's message does not come to us in a progressive, step-by-step format. A glance at the text is enough to highlight repetition and rhetoric, so I will present its message from the following perspectives:

- The First Passover: that means thinking about verses 1–6 and the events they recount, beginning with Israel's first Passover in Egypt, and the Exodus that followed.
- The Last Passover: that means thinking again about verses 1–6, but as if with Jesus and his disciples, singing these words together in the hours before his death.
- The Exodus Completed: our God is the God of verses 7–8. The story is not over until his saving work is complete.

The First Passover

To see the message of Psalm 114 from the perspective of the first Passover, we must go down to Egypt and retrace a familiar path. One day, the LORD said to Abram, 'Go—leave home and country, and I will make you a great nation.' So Abram went, wandering from place to place, getting to know his God, in trials and temptations. The LORD made a covenant with him, renamed him Abraham, and promised him Canaan's land, yet told him that first his offspring would be slaves for four hundred years in a foreign land.

And so it was. Abraham's great grandsons sold their brother, Joseph, into slavery. But God meant it for good. Joseph became ruler over Egypt and the children of Abraham were saved from famine. Pharaoh gave Jacob and his sons the land of Goshen. The years passed. Joseph died. His brothers died. All that generation passed away. But the people multiplied. Then a new king came to power. He had not known Joseph. All these sons of Jacob seemed to him a threat, so he made them slaves. The Egyptians thrashed them, made their lives bitter, and tried to kill their new-born sons.

That's the world we are in at the beginning of Psalm 114—the house of Jacob is among a people of 'strange language'. It's not just that 'it's all Egyptian' to the Israelites—a 'foreign tongue,' so that everything gets lost in translation. Even if they spoke the same language, there would be no understanding. Whatever the tongue, Pharaoh, 'with his horrid crew,' could only speak the language of fear and tyranny, state and empire, but Israel spoke the language of faith. That's the language Joseph spoke on his deathbed when he said, 'God will surely visit you, and you will carry up my bones from here' (Gen. 50:25). Egypt trusts in Pharaoh to protect them and preserve their land; Israel hopes in God to deliver them and give them a better country. This is double oppression; yes physical, but also spiritual. They live, not just under the crack of the whip, but also the lash of the tongue. Little wonder the people 'groaned' and cried to God for rescue. God heard. God remembered his covenant. God saw. God knew (Exod. 2:24–5).

How so? For sure, their cry came up to God. But God was not ignorant of their plight. He did not need an update. Even before they cry out, God sees; God knows. How does he see? How does he know? He sees and he knows because he is there with them. 'Judah was his sanctuary, Israel his dominion' (v. 2). Judah, Israel, the house of Jacob, are all ways of speaking of God's people. Pharaoh sits on his throne and extends his dominion, but where is the God of Psalm 113, who dwells on high? He is making himself low, establishing a sanctuary for himself among the poor Israelites, seemingly allowing Israel—'his dominion'—

to come under the dominion of a genocidal tyrant. He sees. He knows. They groan. And does his Spirit not groan with them?

Does Pharaoh have any idea what he is trying to do? He sees Israel as a threat, so he oppresses them. But he has no real understanding of the threat. Though he supposes he merely oppresses a people, he attempts to suppress their God. Huge mistake! You can shackle God's people, but their God wears no fetters. The more Pharaoh oppressed Israel, the more they multiplied. Yet the tyrant does not get it. He becomes harder and harder, displaying his kingly might, while Israel's God seems to get smaller and smaller. Is he a God who hides himself? If he is, he hides himself so that his glory and power will be more visible in the salvation of his people.

That is how it will be here. Pharaoh cannot contain God, nor stall omnipotence. He cannot annul the LORD's covenant, nor break his resolve. God will start to show himself; yet plague after plague will not break Pharaoh. The people of Israel will eat their first Passover meal with the blood of the lamb sprinkled on their doorposts, so that when the LORD comes in judgment, he will pass over their houses to strike all the firstborn of Egypt. That is what it took to make Pharaoh relent. But it was no repentance. It was regret—regret that lasted no longer than Israel's circuitous journey to the sea, which is where we are in verse 3. They are not at the Red Sea because Moses got lost. God took them there, so that, as he says, 'I will get glory over Pharaoh and all his host, and the Egyptians shall know that I am the LORD' (Exod. 14:4). Then with the Egyptians hard on their heels, Moses lifts his staff and divides the sea. God's people walk through and come out on dry land. The Egyptians follow, only for their 'monstrous anger' to be extinguished in a watery grave.

'The sea saw and fled' (v. 3). With these few words, Psalm 114 recalls all the events that brought Israel from slavery in Egypt, to worshipping beside the sea. The point is not just that God has power over all creation, though he does; it is not just that he will go to extraordinary lengths to save his people, though he will; it is that all creation must yield to the LORD when he appears to save his people: 'The sea saw and fled.' But is that just about the Red Sea? Perhaps not. Scripture often associates the sea with wickedness and with Satan. And Psalm 114 may be giving the hint that this victory, and Israel's exodus from Egypt, is about a greater conquest.

But the psalmist does not stay camped forever at the Red Sea. He goes on to say, 'Jordan turned back.' And with that, he takes us on a huge journey, on to Marah where the people moaned at Moses and he made the bitter waters sweet, on to the wilderness of Sin, where they grumbled again and God gave them manna, on to Massah and Meribah where they quarrelled—again—and God gave them water from the Rock, on to Sinai where he gave them the Ten Commandments. All in all, forty years of wandering, grumbling, and sinning. But also forty years of God's faithfulness, patience, and mercy. The LORD has taken Moses from them, but raised up Joshua in his place. And now they stand by the Jordan, waiting to cross into the Promised Land.

The Levitical priests set out first, carrying the ark of the covenant, 2,000 cubits ahead of the people, and when they step into the river, the waters stand still, and the priests stand still, until all Israel passes over Jordan and stands in Canaan. The exodus from Egypt and the crossing of the Red Sea were just the beginning. Even now that Jordan has turned back, it is not the end of the story—'the mountains skipped like rams, the hills like lambs' (v. 4).

Some writers connect this with Mount Sinai when God gave the law,[1] but that was a terrifying moment, which does not fit

1 e.g. Allan Harman, *Psalms*, Vol. 2 (Fearn: Mentor, 2011), 814; J. J. Stewart Perowne, *The Book of Psalms*, Vol. II (London: Bell & Daldy, 1868), 276.

with the idea of playful lambs. The Psalm does not take us back from the Jordan to Sinai or other historical events, but forward into blessing—blessing so marvellous that he can only use images of mountains and hills skipping and dancing. It is as if Canaan, worn out with the evil of its current inhabitants, jumps and leaps for joy. As Israel steps out of the river, the battered old creation gets a whiff of new creation and reaches out for the people of God. Tabor and Hermon rejoice. Zion cannot contain herself; she breaks into a dance—the LORD has chosen Zion, the ark is coming home, God's children are crossing over Jordan.

So that is the account of what God did at the first Passover. We might expect the psalmist to leave it there. Time to move on! But no, he wants to stand back and take another look, as if to ask, 'Have I grasped it all, have I understood all the implications?' He does that in verses 5–6, using the words of verses 3–4, but turning them into a question: 'Why was it, O sea, that you fled, O Jordan, that you turned back, you mountains, that you skipped like rams, you hills, like lambs?' Speak to us. Tell us what you saw. Were the people of God so terrifying that you fled? Was their arrival truly so wonderful that you skipped and danced? Why was it?

There is only one explanation, and we find it back in verse 2: 'Judah was his sanctuary, Israel his dominion.' The LORD who hid himself among them when they were in slavery, makes himself known when he carries them out of Egypt. He does not put himself on full view, but he allows such a glimpse of his glory and power that creation goes into convulsions of terror and joy—seas retreat, mountains leap. But what now? How must we react? The psalmist is an Old Testament man, so 'that's the end of the story. Moses crossed the Red Sea. Joshua fought the battle of Jericho. Israel settled down in Canaan. And that was that.' Except that is not what he says. Rather this: 'Tremble, O earth, at the presence of the LORD' (v. 7).

'Why?' we might ask, 'That's hardly necessary; it's all over now. Surely you don't think there will be another Exodus? You don't think God will again divide seas or dam rivers?'

'No,' he might respond, 'we're expecting something much bigger. The Exodus, the fleeing sea, the halted Jordan, and everything in between, was just the beginning.'

Why else would he say, 'Tremble, O earth'? His God has not retired. The LORD still dwells with his people. And he will reveal himself again, only in greater power and majesty. 'Tremble, O earth.'

The Last Passover

So, were his expectations met? Or are his expectations yet to be met? We can take that question to the last Passover, and consider it, thinking about verses 1–6 as if with Jesus and his disciples, singing together in the hours before his death. Jesus has already sung Psalm 113. He knows he is at the table because the LORD humbles himself to raise the needy from the dunghill. The Father has given him that task. To fulfil it, Jesus knows he must go much lower yet.

But what of Psalm 114? Jesus sings these words first as a believer and a worshipper. During his earthly ministry he has said so much to confirm that. These momentous events were as real for Jesus as they were for the psalmist; he believed and praised his God and Father for those miraculous deeds. Anyone who cannot join him in that, who cannot believe and worship with him, has a problem not just with the psalmist or with the Old Testament, but with Jesus Christ. The men who sing with Jesus are also believers. They have some understanding of this Psalm's message. They understand that the Exodus from Egypt was only the beginning. Something will happen, and they expect Jesus to be involved. Although they are in the Promised Land, they are not free, yet as John the Baptist's father prophesied, they expect a sunrise from on high. Jesus has told them as much. He will bring the work that God began in the Exodus to a higher level.

But what will Jesus do? What does he expect to do? Throughout his short life he has been searching the Scriptures, and the Holy Spirit has poured himself into Jesus, so that he understands who he is and what he came to do. Not so long ago, he spoke with Moses and Elijah on the mountain about his departure—his exodus. And now, around the Passover table, that moment is almost upon him, yet he is still learning, still growing in wisdom, and gaining a deeper insight into what he is about to suffer and what he is about to achieve. He sings this Psalm, thinking not just of an exodus past, but of an exodus that is about to take place. He knows that in becoming man, he, the eternal Son of God, has already performed an act requiring such power that the dividing of the sea is hardly worth a mention. The God who made Judah his sanctuary, who saw and who knew their groaning, has come lower still—low enough to feel our infirmities and to face every temptation.

But what next for Jesus? How will Psalm 114's expectations come to fulfilment? Jesus will tell his disciples as they recline at this table. As they are eating, Jesus takes bread, blesses it, breaks it, and gives it to the disciples saying, 'Take, eat; this is my body, which is given for you, do this in remembrance of me.' And after supper, he will take the cup, saying, 'This cup is the new covenant in my blood, which is shed for you.' He could have done that at any mealtime with his disciples, but he leaves it until this last Passover because he wants them to understand that his exodus is the exodus that really matters.

Back at the first Passover, the blood of many lambs sprinkled on many doorposts meant that the angel passed over. Now Jesus is the Lamb. His shed blood will save his people from their sins. After they have sung the last hymn, Psalm 118, Jesus will go out to face an enemy greater than Pharaoh, and a river deeper than Jordan. He will battle Satan; the waters will come into his soul. This is the real Exodus. Moses stood on the seashore bearing no scars. Our Lord Jesus will stand on heaven's shore showing us nail-pierced hands and feet, the battle over, his enemy shackled in fathomless depths.

Like the psalmist, we should now stand back and take another look, as if to ask, 'Have I grasped it all?' Ask, why was it? Why, O earth, did you go into convulsions? Why did darkness cover the whole land and the veil of the temple split? Why did the earth shake and rocks split apart? Why was it as if creation wanted to flee away? Ask these men who were at the table with Jesus: Why was it? And they, now apostles, would tell us, 'It was because *God* was in Christ reconciling the world to himself. What men were too blind to see, soulless creation could not ignore. And when we, his disciples, fell silent the very stones had to cry out. And do not think that there is no more to come. This is still the message: "Tremble, O earth, at the presence of the LORD." The work of Christ is done. His exodus is complete. But the universe has yet to encounter the full implications of his victory.'

The Exodus Completed

That is why, not even now can we go beyond verses 7–8. It is still the church's task to say, 'Tremble, O earth at the presence of the LORD, at the presence of the God of Jacob.' Where is the God of Jacob today? He is where he always was, back in verses 1–2, with the house of Jacob, in his sanctuary, dwelling with his people, inhabiting his church. And that has profound implications for the whole earth.

Oxford University's Future of Humanity Institute recently produced, 'a scientific assessment about the possibility of oblivion,' which highlighted twelve ways civilization could end. Stuart Armstrong, a research fellow at the Institute says that 'Putting the risk of extinction [within the next 100 years] below 5 per cent would be wildly overconfident.'[2] But in their focus on super volcanoes, an artificial intelligence takeover, or whatever else, Oxford's academics miss the greatest threat to the earth as we know it—not superbugs or asteroids, but the church of Jesus Christ, or more specifically, the God of Jacob dwelling with his people and inhabiting his church.

The situation is as unsustainable as Israel's captivity in Egypt. Life on earth cannot go on like this. God cannot be suppressed. He will break out to set his people free, with earth-shattering consequences. Consider God's sanctuary today, the church that Christ inhabits; where is it? A great part of it is in heaven—in another dimension, so near but yet so far, where saints, many of whom we have known, behold the Lamb. Another part of the church is on earth—a great company of people across the nations who love our Lord Jesus. But even the church in paradise has considerable interests in this earth. All but a couple of the saints above left their bodies here. And our Lord Jesus will not rest; his completeness cannot be divorced from the completeness of his church (Eph. 1:23). Not only must his people be together in one place—the church in heaven and on earth combined—they must be together in the body, raised from the dust with transformed bodies like his glorious body.

What the first Exodus anticipated, Christ's exodus will achieve. He became the Lamb to make that happen. For most Christians, a day will come when we are laid in earth. How long we will lie there no one knows. But the Lord Jesus marks the spot where his loved ones lie, and he will come again to wake us when the day dawns. If he needs to, he will tear the whole universe apart to gather our dust and raise us up in glory. In a way, that is exactly what he will do. When the New Testament

2 Clive Cookson, '12 Ways the World Could End' in *FT Weekend Magazine*, 14 February 2015, 40.

alludes to Psalm 114 in Revelation 20:11,[3] it has that final day in view, anticipating the moment when not only seas will flee from the presence of the LORD, but also earth and sky. These last few verses of Revelation 20 lay out the full implications of the psalmist's theology.

John sees 'a great white throne.' Dazzling whiteness and blinding brightness say you cannot approach. Here is a seat of such purity and perfection, holiness and separation that just to look at it is practically impossible. And it's vast—so great in its all-eclipsing enormity that by comparison nothing else appears to exist. This is the seat of absolute power, 'the throne of God and of the Lamb' (Rev. 22:1). Now is the moment Jesus promised in Matthew 25, when he would burst back into creation, not as an incognito king, but on this throne, and in such an explosion of glory that every eye shall see him. Nothing can be the same again. The events of Revelation 20:11–15 become unstoppable. The words of verse 11 now sum up the history of the universe: 'No place was found for them.' Why this great displacement? Why has 'earth and sky fled from his presence'? What is it that soulless creation cannot ignore this time? We could ask the psalmist's question: 'What ails you … that you flee?'

But there is no time for questions. We see the great white throne—'the presence of the LORD'—and in that instant the universe is gone. In the beginning, God created, but at the moment of deliverance and judgment it is as if all creation wants to be unmade—scarred and marred by human sin, this earth with its accursed ground, and these heavens, like tormented witnesses to the evil of a thousand generations, flee from his holy presence.

That also means the end of every social, intellectual, religious, and political refuge. The world expressed its rebellion against

3 Nestle-Aland, 'Loci citati vel allegati' in *Novum Testamentum Graece.* (Stuttgart: Deutsche Bibelgesellschaft, 1993), 787.

the LORD and his anointed through the hardened Pharaohs of many nations, through powerful institutions and great movements, through profound philosophies and carefully-constructed views of reality. In them, men and women took refuge, but in a moment all is gone—vanished with the fleeing creation. 'No place is found for them.'

Whenever this moment will come, it will come in answer to the groans and cries of God's people. From the psalmist's day to that last Passover with Jesus, those who waited for 'the consolation of Israel' never doubted that the Exodus from Egypt foretokened a greater exodus. And from Christ's day until the end of time, they never doubted that his exodus was the first-fruits of new creation. When we see the great white throne, and creation forever displaced, then shall we know that God is about to give us our hearts' desires. God sees. God knows. He comes to save his people and to bring in the new creation, which necessarily means he also comes to judge the world.

And so he does. If creation is displaced, then so are the dead. You see them too in Revelation 20:12–14. 'No place was found for them' either. The displaced dead have nowhere to go. Generation after generation looked for security in this world and in what can be seen—a home, a family, a job, a place in the community. Their leaders promised them such security—a better future, economic stability, peace and safety. Even in the church, many worshippers and leaders looked for security in this world, in being recognised and praised, applauded and commended. But they all died. Most of them hoped that this life is all there is, that the grave is the end and there they would be at peace under the everlasting protection of the world in which they trusted. In a sense, they rested in peace; dead bodies suffer no pain. But does this earth give her dead any more security than she gives to her living? In the end, she deserts us all; at the presence of the God of Jacob, the earth and the heavens flee away, taking no one with them.

So this is inevitable: 'And I saw the dead, the great and the small, standing before the throne' (Rev. 20:12). All humanity, by creation now deserted, by the world in which it trusted—abandoned. In this, the exodus proper, not even the sea is hospitable: 'The sea gave up the dead that were in it, and death and Hades gave up the dead that were in them' (Rev. 20:13). What else can the universe do but vomit up its dead? Their dust and bones belong not to the earth, but to God, so the earth must give them back before she flees. The dead will make a final plea to her, calling to the mountains and rocks, 'Fall on us and hide us from the face of him who is seated on the throne' (Rev. 6:16)—'Give us our graves back! Don't forsake us now!' A futile plea; earth and heavens have fled away. No place was found for them, so no place is found for the dead. They must stand before the presence of the LORD—exposed, displaced, undone, raised to a fully-conscious, re-embodied experience of death, existing now in a place of non-existence.

What can we say to all that? How should we respond to the message of Psalm 114—'Tremble, O earth'? Shall we resist it? Many do. Reject it? They do that too. Whatever the response, the church can only turn and say, 'Tremble, O earth, at the presence of the LORD.' There is only one fitting response, which is to join the generations of God's people, and sing these words with them, with all Israel, with Jesus, and with the church. They sing this song not just in words, but through lives shaped by this expectation, that we will see him again when the new creation skips for joy and reaches out for the people of God.

That may seem to be a long time in coming, and when we reflect on our lives, we have to confess that we are much shaped by the concerns of this life, and too much like the Israelites, complaining against God's providence and against his exit strategy for his people, asking, 'God, what on earth are you doing? Why have you brought us into this mess?' The final verse of the psalm is for people like us, people like the Israelites in Exodus 17, thirsty and complaining, until God told Moses to strike the rock and water flowed out. We struggle to walk by faith and not by sight. We think we know what we need and when we need it better than God. But see what miracles the LORD performs, even for grumbling rebels—he turns the flint into springs of water.

Whatever I think I need, my greatest need is to drink from these springs—springs that always pointed to something greater. As Paul says in 1 Corinthians 10:4, '…the Rock was Christ.' That is why Jesus could say, 'Whoever drinks of the water that I shall give him will never thirst' (John 4:14). That is what Christ's Exodus brings for his people. He does not rescue us only to let us die of thirst, nor does he deliver us only to have us battle the waves alone. He takes us home to rejoice in his victory beside the sea of glass.

So what are we to make of Psalm 114? What does exodus finally mean for God's people? This: 'They shall hunger no more, neither thirst anymore…the Lamb who is in the midst of the throne will shepherd them, and shall lead them to springs of living water, and God will wipe away every tear from their eyes' (Rev. 7:16–17).

5

TRUST IN THE LORD

Psalm 115

Sometimes depression follows elation. Low mood chases away the satisfaction of a big event. Post-holiday blues or post-retirement blues take hold. Psalm 115 is for people determined to resist such gloom, specifically post-Exodus blues.

This was the third Hallel Psalm for Israel to sing during the Passover meal as they remembered how God delivered them from Egypt. By now, those at the table have sung of their exalted LORD humbling himself to raise the poor from the dust (Ps. 113), and of creation taking fright when he rescued their forefathers from Egypt (Ps. 114). With expectant hearts, they said, 'Tremble, O earth at the presence of the LORD' (114:8). But what if many setbacks, even exile from the land of promise, have made their Passovers forlorn memorials?—

'We said, "Tremble, O earth," but the presence of the LORD is nowhere to be seen. The day is as dark as we feel gloomy. And can you blame us? Have you heard what the nations are

[1] Not to us LORD, not to us,
but to your name give glory
for the sake of your loving-kindness and faithfulness.

[2] Why should the nations say,
'Where is their God?'
[3] But our God is in heaven;
He does all that he pleases.

[4] Their idols are silver and gold,
the work of men's hands.
[5] They have mouths, but do not speak;
they have eyes, but do not see;
[6] they have ears, but do not hear;
they have noses, but do not smell;
[7] hands, but they do not feel;
feet, but they do not walk;
nor do they make a sound through their throats.

[8] Their makers are like them;
so are all who trust in them.

[9] O Israel, trust in the LORD;
he is their help and shield.
[10] House of Aaron, trust in the LORD;
he is their help and shield.
[11] You who fear the LORD, trust in the LORD;
he is their help and shield.

[12] The LORD has remembered us,
he will bless us,
he will bless the house of Israel;
he will bless the house of Aaron.
[13] he will bless those who fear the LORD—
both small and great.

[14] May the LORD give you increase, you and your children.
[15] May you be blessed by the LORD,
who made heaven and earth.
[16] The heaven of heavens is the LORD's,
but he has given earth to men's sons.

[17] The dead do not praise the LORD,
nor those who go down to silence.

[18] But we will bless the LORD,
from now and for evermore.

Hallelujah.

saying (v. 2)? "Where is their God?" In fact, we've been asking that ourselves.'

The Christian church should sympathize. We recall a greater victory, won not at the Red Sea, but at Golgotha. We call on our world to tremble at the presence of Christ, but the nations have questions. Peter sums them up: 'Where is the promise of his coming? For ever since the fathers fell asleep, all things are continuing as they were from the beginning of creation' (2 Pet. 3:4). And we admit, all things are indeed continuing as they were. If anything, beyond the spin and self-affirmation, the church in the Western world grows weaker. Where is the presence of the LORD? We have our own post-Calvary blues.

Psalm 115 should change our outlook. With several alternating voices, it may appear confusing, but the psalmist's goal is clear. Verses 9–11 repeat his central exhortation three times: 'Trust in the LORD.' That is hardly eye-grabbing therapy for morose believers who might prefer a more elaborate treatment plan—seven steps to happiness, ten keys to unlocking your joy, or twenty-four habits of victorious Christians. But believers only need to count to one. One trait will take them even to the better country: 'Trust in the LORD.'

Some detect complex structures in Psalm 115, but if the repeated call to 'trust in the LORD' captures the thrust of the Psalm, it is simpler to view it as two halves, giving us two reasons to trust in the LORD.

- Verse 3 best summarises the first half (vv. 1–8). It gives the first reason to trust in the LORD: 'Our God is in heaven.'
- In the second half (vv. 9–18), verse 12 provides a summary statement and the second reason to trust in the LORD: 'The LORD has remembered us.'

This chapter will follow that template, but with a pair of bookends. Because Psalm 115's opening words are often quoted in isolation, it is worth asking beforehand how they integrate with the whole Psalm and its call to trust in the LORD. Then, since Psalm 115 concludes part one of the Hallel, we consider the outlook it offers—'from now and forevermore' (v. 18).

'Not to Us, O Lord'

The psalm's opening words—'Not to us, O LORD, not to us, but to your name give glory'—are probably more famous than the psalm itself. Shakespeare's Henry V announced at Agincourt, 'Let there be sung *Non nobis* [Ps. 115] and *Te Deum*.' What psalm exactly the playwright thought Henry wanted sung before the dead were 'with charity enclosed in clay' may be a matter of discussion,[1] but Shakespeare's account so shapes the English consciousness that Psalm 115 had to be part of Choral Matins broadcast from the Chapel Royal, St James's Palace, on St Crispin's day 2015, the 600th anniversary of Agincourt.[2] Robert Louis Stevenson and Rudyard Kipling likewise gave *Non nobis domine* a line in their poetry, although Kipling's 1934 poem echoes more of the Psalm's content.

Perhaps verse 1 has been amputated like this because it may appear disconnected from what follows, and more suited to what came before in Psalm 114, making it an ideal victors' hymn. Psalm 115's opening words could recall deliverance past, but they do connect with what follows. 'Not to us, O LORD, not to us…' means nothing without 'trust in the LORD.' Trust in him gives him glory; trust denied deprives him of glory. From Exodus to Promised Land, every step forward for Israel was a step of faith; every step backward, a stumble into unbelief that denied him glory and gave it to someone or something else.

1 Naseeb Shaheen, *Biblical References in Shakespeare's Plays* (London: Associated University Presses, 1999), 469–471.

2 www.bbc.co.uk/programmes/b06k9szm [Accessed on-line, 27 Feb. 2016].

Denying God glory and giving it to ourselves need not mean crude self-aggrandisement. Anything less than total trust takes glory from him. Behind the quiet thought that the LORD needs us, or at least our cooperation, lies a glory-denying mind-set. Christians who speak the language of grace-not-works may recoil at the suggestion that we could even think like that. But this way of thinking so pervades the human disposition that our own hearts are sure to introduce us to someone inclined to it. Anyone can speak the language of grace; few become so fluent that they think and dream in it. No one needs spiritual open heart surgery to find the same worm that killed Herod from the inside out waiting to kill us too (Acts 12:21–23). It lurks not so much in our moments of Herodian pride as in our everyday anxieties about universal human concerns.

For Israel, the events of Psalm 114 might indeed more easily awaken a 'Not to us Lord' than what Psalm 115 will recount. We too may instinctively want to glorify the LORD when we think of salvation from sin and death, yet facing the sometimes trivial anxieties of life we struggle to trust in the LORD. And what if that betrays a lack of trust in him for crucial spiritual needs, such as acceptance with him and the hope of forgiveness? This may become most obvious when we ask, 'What motivates me to join in worship, to serve the church, or to resist sin? Is it the fruit of forgiveness, or is it a plea for forgiveness?' If we find that our spiritual and religious activities express not contentment with what God has done, but rather a plea for acceptance with him, then we do not step forward in faith; we stumble into glory-taking unbelief.

For us and for our communities, life after Calvary can be such a disappointment, so we try to reinstate what came before Calvary, or to reverse our unbelief with a ruinous, self-directed, glory-snatching grab for influence (cf. Num. 14:39ff.). At the root of it all is a failure to trust in the LORD, which is always simultaneous with a failure to give him glory. Ever since the LORD brought Abraham outside to count the stars, faith and giving glory to God have waxed and waned together (Rom. 4:20). Psalm 115's opening words declare that conviction. One principle; two expressions. Addressed to God: 'Not to us, O LORD, not to us…' Addressed to man: 'Trust in the LORD.'

The psalm is precise about the object of our glory—'to your name give glory'. While 'the name' of the LORD has the same import as in Psalm 113 (p. 39), in the context of Psalm 115 this statement proclaims that the LORD must have glory on his terms. He is who he is, and who he is, is all in his name. Let him have glory for every aspect of his character, not only for certain 'palatable' characteristics. Yet of them all, the psalmist highlights two—'love and faithfulness'.

Why these two? Would a display of naked power not better magnify his glory to an idolatrous world? No one who recalled Israel's exodus from Egypt could think that. Human beings do not give glory to God when he displays his power. The more God displayed his power, the harder Pharaoh became. To give glory to the LORD for his power is to glorify him for a characteristic that individuals may encounter apart from his covenant love; to give him glory for his love, is to give him glory for all that he does, and for all that his name represents to his people. Even that spectacular display of his power exercised against Pharaoh served his love and faithfulness towards them. When God exercises his love towards his children, he invests his power and wisdom, righteousness and justice, freedom and knowledge—his whole being—in loving them. He holds nothing back. And no one that he loves wants him to hold anything back because his covenant love brings us into a binding relationship with him. To object to the way he loves is to spurn what he is and to strike at the heart of the relationship.

Israel did exactly that in the centuries after the Exodus. The Old Testament records how they tried to cling to the gifts of love, yet spurn the giver. But the whole-being love of their covenant LORD would not let them go. Therefore he says, 'for the sake of your love *and faithfulness.*'—'Give glory to the LORD for his love, exercised in such power when he took us out of Egypt, but give glory also for the way he kept loving even as we spurned him. All day long he held out his hands to us. He took us into exile, not to drive us away, but to heal us. We confess that of our past. His love and faithfulness is our hope for the future. Our trust in the LORD begins here. So we say, "Not to us LORD, not to us, but to your name give glory."'

'Our God Is in Heaven'

That opening statement is, however, challenging as a declaration of hope for the future, especially when hostile onlookers provide a rationale for post-Exodus despair. The nations do that with their taunt, 'Where is their God?' (v. 2). That question gets to God's people when they feel his absence, or when they think, 'He did great things in the past, but he's not doing much now.' What he did in the past becomes not a measure of what he will do in the future, but a testimony to his absence that drives them into a vicious circle of self-reliance.

In the verses that follow, the psalmist shows us how to escape that vortex and how to deal with this cynical question. *First*, wrap it in another question and bring it to the LORD: 'Why should the nations say, "Where is their God?"' Take the question and the abuse to God. Turn their scepticism into prayer. Make an argument of it and say, 'LORD, this makes you look so bad. Why would you do this? Why would you pour out such love to save us only to let us fall? We bear your name. The nations of the world see your face in our circumstances. Why should they say that you are an absentee father?'

The *second* thing to do with the question is to answer it: 'But our God is in heaven; he does all that he pleases' (v. 3). In other words, 'What a stupid question. Imagine asking, "Where is their God?" "Our God is in heaven." What do they expect him to do? Send them a photo? Make an appearance? Give them a wave? Shed a tear? We know exactly where our God is. Though their mockery unsettles us, when we lift our eyes to heaven, we see the invisible, and having seen what they cannot see, we will not go back. For a moment their ridicule might obscure our view, but they cannot blind eyes of faith: Our God is in heaven; he does all that he pleases.

'We long for God to act. We expect it. That's why we said, "Tremble, O earth." We believe the Exodus was only the beginning. His covenant love and faithfulness will always endure. Yet sometimes we wonder why he acts as he does. Why does he hide himself? Why are his saving ways so strange? Sometimes we see his wise purpose, but we are often dumfounded. Yet somehow we find every mystery resolved when we lift our eyes to heaven, and with humbled minds and trusting hearts, we say, "He does whatever pleases him."'

Verses 4–8 set out the *third* way the psalmist deals with the question. He almost fires it back at them. 'The nations say of us, "Where is their God?" so let's ask them the same question, "Where is your god?" Whatever you do, don't look up; their god is not in heaven; their gods are much more manageable. Like children with a snowman, they make their gods out of silver and gold. They give them eyes, ears, and noses, hands, feet, and throats. Surely if you create something, it should worship you. Not for these creators. Their gods see nothing, hear nothing, smell nothing, and do nothing. They go nowhere. They do not say a word. In fact, their gods are not merely mute, but dead.

'Yet these nations trust those idols. They can see their gods, but what have they ever seen their gods do for them? Not a thing. They do everything for their gods, yet they have the hard neck to say of us, "Where is their God?" These people are as dumb, stupid, and dead as their gods. "Their makers are like them, so are all who trust in them"' (v. 8).

None of this is remote from our day. Psalm 115 highlights a consistent distinction between 'our God' and 'their gods'—they cannot see 'our God', but we can see theirs. Even if invisible demonic and spiritual powers control idolatry, idolatrous religions consistently express themselves in what is seen—'the work of men's hands' (v. 4). In some religions the 'work of men's hands' is still an idol on a pedestal, but for others, the idol is the religious institution itself, or the privilege and influence that belonging to the religion may bring. 'Idols and their worshippers...mimic true divine revelation,'[3] and often do it so well that their mimicry is almost indiscernible from the real thing. Even so, their mimicry cannot stop them gravitating towards the seen: worshippers and their leaders still cling to the visible. Under such subtle apostasty, superficially pure, orthodox churches succumb to idolatry as they venerate human resources: churches confuse financial sustainability and numerical growth (or the lack of it) with divine approval, or they look to modern media to win a lost generation ('media idolatry'[4]), producing adherents whose faith leans on impressive leaders and their reciprocal endorsements.

Such idolatry is as difficult to unravel in ourselves as it is in our institutions. We say, 'Our God is in heaven,' yet we cannot hide our need to be liked, off-line or on-line. In her book *Vainglory*, DeYoung writes of people 'starved for unconditional love... checking the "like" versus "dislike" counts on...Facebook posts for an ego boost several times a day.'[5] If this is vainglory, it is also idolatry and a grasping for security in something other

3 See Daniel Strange, *'For Their Rock Is not as Our Rock': An evangelical theology of religions* (Nottingham: Apollos, 2014), 247. Also his account of other religions as idolatrous counterfeiters of true divine revelation, 246–59.

4 See D. Brent Laytham, *iPod, YouTube, Wii Play: Theological Engagements with Entertainment* (Eugene: Cascade Books, 2012), 20–22.

5 Rebecca Konyndyk DeYoung, *Vainglory: The Forgotten Vice* (Grand Rapids, Eerdmans, 2014), 120.

than the LORD. Cyber-friends or institutions bestow upon us some this-worldly significance, but what happens when the cycle of mutual affirmation is broken? What if we are stripped of all visible reference points? Will the stark conviction, 'Our God is in heaven', be enough?

We should not avoid such questions. Where you place your trust, what you cling to for security, seen or unseen: Behold your god! In home and family, in financial prudence or intellectual frameworks, in scientific advances or political ideals, in status and position, in so many praiseworthy things coerced into idolatrous service, men and women place their trust. Through this legion of gods they worship the creature rather than the Creator. They think all their needs are met until at the end of their lives they find their gods impotent to help them face down their greatest fear. Yet even in their final moments, few abandon their vanishing gods. Despite the certain knowledge that such seen gods can do nothing, human beings trust more easily in them than in an unseen God, who does whatever he pleases. 'Their makers are like them.' Blind, deaf, and silent. Dead.

Was it easy for our Lord Jesus to sing those words as death approached? We cannot suppose he took up the words of this Psalm at the Last Passover with triumphalistic relish. After all, 'no one ever feared death so much as this Man.'[6] Compared to the Saviour, the psalmist enjoyed spiritual luxuries. He could take the nations' question and stamp it, 'Return to Sender.' When the nations asked, 'Where is their God?' the believing people of God could deal with the question in that way too. Not Jesus. He will not escape such taunting (Matt. 27:43).

6 Cranfield's reserved rendering of Luther's perhaps more emotive statement: '*Sed est propter nos factum*, Das der man so hoch betrubt *ut nullus homo, et nullus* so hoch fur dem tod gefurcht...'. C. E. B. Cranfield, *The Apostle's Creed* (London: Continuum, 2004), 34; Luther's Werke, vol. 37 (Weimar: Hermann Böhlaus Nachfolger, 1910), 326. Also MacLeod, *Person of Christ*, 174.

That sneering question will pursue him through the hours of darkness until it becomes all-consuming and immovable as he submits to the abandonment of death (Matt. 27:46).

And what of the answer? 'But our God is in heaven; he does all that he pleases' (v. 3). How could Jesus sing, 'He does all that he pleases'? Could he sing? It would be no shame if he were too overcome to open his mouth. Soon God's pleasure will take him down into the realm of mute and blind insentience destined for idolaters. Not that he judges himself a tragic man about to be slain by darkness 'because he did the wrong thing in the wrong place at the wrong time.'[7] He knows Isaiah's prophecy, 'Yet it pleased the LORD to bruise him; he has put him to grief' (53:10). So he sorrows and sweats, but still he trusts in the LORD: 'O my Father, if it be possible, let this cup pass from me; nevertheless, not as I will, but as you will' (Matt. 26:39). He could pray like that because he took Psalm 115 to heart, and in doing so, he showed us how to trust in the LORD, who 'does all that he pleases.' He shows us how to pray, not that we may upend God's eternal purposes or change his will, but so that we may be conformed perfectly to his will, and nurture this trust-filled attitude: 'not as I will, but as you will.'

'The Lord Has Remembered Us'

The next half of the Psalm (vv. 9–18) lays down a second ground for trust in the LORD: 'He has remembered us.' Verses 9–11 clasp the two halves together. The call to trust in the LORD comes to all of God's people: 'O Israel… house of Aaron… you who fear the LORD.' This is Psalm 113's vision of a people of God that will stretch beyond Jacob's sons. Psalm 115 likewise sweeps aside all limited expectations when it says again: 'those

7 Geza Vermes, *Searching for the Real Jesus: Jesus, the Dead Sea Scrolls and Other Religious Themes* (London: SCM Press, 2009), 24.

who fear the LORD—both small and great' (v. 13). The psalmist has an eye on a great multitude, who seeing the impotence of idols, count themselves hopeless without the LORD's love. They seek the help of a self-emptying God and the protection of a redeeming LORD, so he stands eager to welcome all of them to his congregation, exhorting and assuring: 'Trust in the LORD; he is their help and shield.'

This assembly needs no warmup. Wooden responsories have no place in the liturgy. These few words call forth a stream of confident declaration, 'He will bless… He will bless… He will bless… He will bless…' (vv. 12–13). Our God, they say, will do what idols can never do; 'He will bless us.' Blessing has a source never to be found in a mindless idol. It springs from divine mindfulness: 'The LORD has remembered us' (v. 12). If this were a bare forensic recollection of all that we are it would be no blessing, but the LORD remembers us according to the covenant love and faithfulness with which the psalm began (v. 1). That places *not* remembering at the heart of his remembering (cf. Ps. 25:7; Jer. 31:20, 34), which opens the way for unlimited blessing. If the LORD has remembered us, what else do we need? How far will his remembering take you? All the way to paradise. If he does nothing else but remember you, all will be well. The dying thief understood that much: 'Jesus, remember me when you come into your kingdom' (Luke 23:42). When the LORD remembers his people, he blesses his people, and the blessing he commands is, as another Psalm points out, nothing less than life that shall never end (Ps. 133:3).

As the psalmist moves on, he can barely contain himself (vv. 14–16). Anyone who did not know his God would think him delusional: increase—God's people growing in numbers, blessing—extending to children's children, irrepressible life grabbing hold of the next generation. And why not? The LORD made heaven and earth; what can he not do? He dwells in the heaven of heavens, but he has given us the earth; what could he not give? Our God is no dead idol who needs us to bestow significance upon him or affirm his existence. The flow of significance and meaning comes from him to us. He is the source and giver of life. He gives the life to those he blesses, and he will never take it from those he remembers. Anxiety-free, glory-giving trust in the LORD rests upon this.

No post-Exodus blues now. Trust drove them into the sea. God's people have put the misery of a glory-denying mindset behind them. 'Not to us LORD, not to us…' has become a statement of living faith and obedient trust in the LORD. But do the words of verse 17, 'the dead do not praise the LORD, nor those who go down to silence,' fit with this positive new outlook? What happened to the blessing and irrepressible life? They are still there for those who trust the LORD, but verse 17 gives a final or summary comparison with those who place their security in idols. Since Psalm 113, the LORD has been raising his people up, out of death and bondage, into a world of praise and celebration. They will bless the LORD, now and forevermore (v. 18), as Psalm 113:2 predicted. The dead, on the other hand, these worshippers of dumb idols, must go in the other direction —away from the LORD and his life-giving blessing. Into silence. Away from their noise and self-made joys. They never sung a true 'Hallelujah' in this life, and they never will.

If it ever seems that post-redemption blues are not so easily banished and that the trust to drive them away does not come so readily, we should again remember Jesus. Think again of the dying thief, and then of Christ's reply, 'Today, you will be with me in Paradise' (Luke 23:43). Which of these two men had the greatest faith? The thief, or Jesus? The thief surely had faith, but not like Jesus' faith. It took greater faith for Christ to say, 'Today, you will be with me in Paradise,' than for the thief to say, 'Remember me.' Jesus hangs in God-forsaken exile, rejected and reviled, yet even there he has the faith to say to his fellow-man, 'Today, you will be with me in Paradise.'

How could Jesus do that? He could do it because he trusted in God. The message of Psalm 115 had shaped his holy character. Now, even in the night, he trusts in God, not seeking his own glory, but the glory of the LORD who sent him, so that his covenant love and faithfulness will be magnified as never before. Our Lord Jesus clings to his Father even as he bruises him, so that many more will sing, 'But we will bless the LORD, from now and forevermore' (v. 18). Whether I can sing that depends upon where I find my security and where I place my trust. Will I go down to silence, or will I worship in the great congregation? It depends where I bow the knee today.

Now and Forevermore

Our introduction to the great congregation came in the opening verses of Psalm 113, with its vision of worship 'from now and forevermore,' and 'from the rising of the sun to the place where it sets.' The first half of the Hallel (113–115), calls the LORD's people to united worship and praise, so it is fitting that at the end of Psalm 115 we should see that congregation in its final, transnational, eternal fullness. Scripture itself opens up such a vista when, in Revelation, Jesus Christ draws on the Hallel 'to show his servants the things which must soon take place' (Rev. 1:1). Many students of the Apocalypse detect an 'unmistakable'[8] reference to those Psalms in Revelation 19:5. The longed-for congregation of Psalm 113 has become 'a great multitude in heaven' (Rev. 19:1), called to worship with a medley of Psalms 113:1 and 115:13 (Rev. 19:5), which recalls the

8 Massey H. Shepherd, *The Paschal Liturgy and the Apocalypse* (Richmond: John Knox Press, 1960), 96; Alan F. Johnson, 'Revelation' in Expositors Bible Commentary, ed. Frank E. Gaebelein [Pradis 5.01.0035] (Grand Rapids: Zondervan, 2002). Similarly, John Sweet, *Revelation* (London: SCM Press Ltd, 1979), 277; Ben Witherington III, *Revelation* (Cambridge: Cambridge University Press, 2003), 232; Jonathan Knight, *Revelation* (Sheffield: Sheffield Academic Press, 1999), 125.

whole, and finds in Psalm 115 a fitting doxology to celebrate the eternal impact of Christ's work.

Revelation 19 draws us in from the fringe of a great crowd (vv. 1–3), into the inner circle (v. 4), and finally to the centre of everything—the throne of heaven (v. 5). John's switch from his typical 'After this I saw...' to 'After this I heard...' suggests sound overwhelms sight at the roar of this multitude in heaven, than which until now there has been no greater multitude. Their thundering 'Hallelujah!' (v. 1) is as surprising as it is familiar. After the many Hallelujahs of Psalms 113–118, and the Hallelujahs that follow in other Psalms, down to the last words of the last Psalm (150:6), there are no more Hallelujahs. The Old Testament and the Gospels, the Acts of the apostles, and their epistles proclaim no Hallelujahs—until now. Scripture's final author saved 'Hallelujah' for this day of glory and victory. At the end of time, the pent up praises of every generation explode into an irrepressible 'Hallelujah!' as the heavenly chorus seizes upon the themes of Psalms 113–115 to celebrate the LORD's poor-exalting, enemy-crushing works of saving power, now fulfilled in Jesus Christ and implemented fully on this day.

No one in this great multitude thinks they stand there thanks to the power of man or the glory of any idol. They are the same company who stand beside the sea of glass and sing the song of Moses (Rev. 15) because their exodus from a world of death is an event of the same nature as the Exodus from Egypt—only the LORD could have done it. Standing on the threshold of the new world, they speak the same language as Israel. When Israel remembered God's saving work in Psalm 114, they went on to sing in Psalm 115, 'Not to us, O LORD, not to us, but to your name give glory.' Is that not what this multitude are saying as this shout now goes up, 'Hallelujah! Salvation and glory and power belong to our God'? For them too, the LORD's saving power and glory are most visible in his judgments (v. 2): 'He has judged the great prostitute, who corrupted the earth with her immorality.'

Although this great harlot is synonymous with Babylon, who for the first recipients of Revelation unveiled herself as the Roman empire, she did not restrict her charms to Roman emperors, or to those who called them 'Lord'. She corrupts the whole earth. That much is clear in Revelation 18. All who nestled in her bosom, governments and business, the holders of political, military, and economic power, weep over her destruction. All their security was in her. Without her they are nothing. This tragic woman represents the world order in its rebellion against God. Her clients are all those whose security lies in what they possess, or in the place they have in society. Any life lived not in service to God is a life lived enthralled with her charms. This great whore takes everything you have and leaves you standing naked on her doorstep. Worse than that, she takes her clients down into silence with her when this world with its glory is made desolate 'in one hour' (Rev. 18:19).

In Revelation 19, that hour has passed, so the great multitude praises God for this final judgment; the great prostitute is out of work. She corrupts the earth and sheds the blood of God's servants no more, which as the Venerable Bede pointed out around 1,300 years ago, 'encompasses all the transgression of the wicked.'[9] The relationship between the great prostitute and those she corrupts was a true joint enterprise. Corrupter and corrupted are one. Every prostitute takes something beautiful and puts it to an evil use. The great harlot likewise took a beautiful world and put it to an evil use, persuading her clients that God's good gifts had value apart from him. Together, the corrupter and the corrupted, the world and its inhabitants, reduced the meaning and purpose of life to possessing things,

9 Bede, *Commentary on Revelation*, trans. Faith Wallis (Liverpool: Liverpool University Press, 2013), 243.

achieving ambitions, and enjoying experiences. There is one word for all this—idolatry. The old world was full of idols, so many beautiful things that people put to an evil use, and in which they placed their trust.

Such idolatry, as Psalm 115 says, produces a people who end up just like their idols, facing death, destruction, and decay. Their idolatry inevitably victimized others, but God has now avenged the blood of his servants, which is why the twenty-four elders and the four living creatures fall down and worship God (v. 4). The twenty-four elders are the twelve sons of Jacob and the twelve apostles, representing the whole church in every age. As idolatrous Babylon falls under judgment, the church falls down in worship. In the declensions and transgressions of ancient Israel, in the apostasy and backsliding of the Christian church, the elders have often witnessed the great whore drawing the LORD's people into idolatry. But the LORD has set his people free, so the elders are now men of few words, almost silent before the majesty of God, content to affirm God's judgments and concur with the multitude: 'Amen, Hallelujah!'

Is this their last Amen? Through the ages they have knelt before the throne as representatives of the church. But after this final day the church needs no such representatives because the Hallel's expectation is fulfilled. In this multitude stands every child of God—the whole church gathered home. In that sense, perhaps this is the elders' final bow, a last Amen before they step back to stand with the great multitude and forever join their Hallelujahs to theirs.

Verse 5 brings us to the centre of all things and to the throne of heaven. Now all heaven falls silent, until a voice comes from the throne, saying: 'Praise our God, all you his servants, you who fear him, both small and great!' Who speaks? Not one of the living creatures or an elder. Not God himself because he says, 'our God.' Whoever speaks knows those words, yet is on the throne. This is the voice of the Lamb in the centre of the throne, of the Jesus who in Revelation 3 spoke of 'my God'. It is not incongruous that he should now say 'our God,' because he stands as our great representative, a true man, ready to lead us in praise and to present us to God.

It is as if he says, 'Friends, the last time I sang these words I was with some of you around the Passover table. That night I sang by faith, anticipating an exodus that would take me and you from bondage to glory in my Father's house. And, Hallelujah, here we are gathered from every nation and generation, before the throne and beside the springs of living water. See how the words of Psalm 115 have been fulfilled before our eyes. Those who put their trust in idols have become like them. They have gone down to silence, to a land where no one sings Hallelujah.

'But I, Israel's truest son and greatest priest, trusted in the LORD; he is our help and shield.

'You who fear him trusted in him; he is our help and shield.

'At that Last Passover I sang by faith. You sang by faith thereafter. And the Lord has remembered us. He has blessed us. So let us bless him, from now and forevermore, singing by sight what we sang by faith that night:

Praise our God, all you his servants,
you who fear him,
both small and great!

'I Will Declare Your Name to My Brethren'

Interlude on Hebrews 2

During the Passover meal, the pouring of the fourth cup brought a break in the Hallel between Psalms 114 and 115 (see p. 7). It might have been no less fitting if a pause came between Psalms 115 and 116 where the Hallel switches from the corporate to the personal, so this interlude comes at that point. It will expand on the idea mentioned in chapter two that the worship-leading of Israel's king reaches its enduring highpoint in Jesus Christ. The appearance of Psalms 113 and 115 in Revelation 19 have given an example of this and the second part of the Hallel will reveal more, but it is worth pausing to consider Hebrews 2, which is often given as an example of the principle that Christ leads his people in worship. Hebrews uses a different part of the Psalter to make the point, while retaining a focus on similar themes, not least the theme of trust in God.

It is not difficult to imagine that the recipients of Hebrews, upon hearing the preacher's lofty description of the Son (1:1–14), might well have felt a disjunction between that account and their experience: their Saviour, this eternally-begotten Son, radiating all the glory of the godhead, outranking angels and archangels, loving righteousness and hating wickedness, this all-subduing conqueror, is all but invisible. Anticipating the problem, the preacher says, 'But we do not yet see all things put under him' (2:8), and then gives this seemingly paradoxical answer to the problem: 'we see Jesus' (2:9).

The outstanding feature of Hebrews 2:5–9 is its quotation of Psalm 8, and when we recall the whole psalm in that context, these verses in Hebrews explain how the tension between what we confess and what we experience is resolved when we see Jesus made lower than the angels, *before* he is crowned with glory and honour. Every tension between faith and sight is somehow resolved when we see Jesus.

It is possible, however, to believe that, yet still ask, 'How do I put that into practice?' The second half of Hebrews 2 gives an immediate answer as it expounds verses 5–9. In verse 13, the author hears Jesus say: 'I will put my trust in him.' His burden is that we should do likewise and say of Christ himself, 'I will put my trust in him,' particularly to lead us to God (vv. 10–13) and to deliver us from death (v. 15).

His leading us to God is most relevant to this book. It should go without saying that you cannot just trust anyone to lead you to God. The way someone does that must be acceptable to God, or as Hebrews puts it, 'fitting' (v. 10). It was fitting for Jesus to identify with sinful people simply because in leading many sons to glory he was making Psalm 8's lofty expectations a reality, not just for himself, but for many sons. We can trust him to lead all his sons to glory because he, the captain of our salvation, has himself been made perfect through suffering. Nothing can separate us from him: 'He who sanctifies and those who are being sanctified are all of one' (Heb. 2:11). This salvation has God's full approval. He is the source of it, and now he is altogether satisfied with the sanctifier and the sanctified.

No surprise then that Christ is not ashamed to call them brethren. How could he be ashamed of an outcome so pleasing to his Father? His is not an unashamedness that flies in the face of all the facts. Truly, he is not ashamed. He has no concern that his high expectations for us may yet be dashed or that he will have to disown us. He knows that as surely as he is not ashamed to call them brethren, his Father is not ashamed to call them sons.

Hebrews 2:12–13 tells us how and when Christ calls us brethren:

> *saying: 'I will declare Your name to My brethren;*
> *In the midst of the assembly I will sing praise to You.'*
> *and again: 'I will put My trust in Him.'*
> *And again: 'Here am I*
> *and the children whom God has given Me.'*

Once again, our Lord Jesus takes ownership of Scripture, particularly Psalm 22:22, with Isaiah 8:17 and 18. Together these passages tell us something about the progress of our leader from humiliation to exaltation. If we were to take them in chronological order, we would probably begin in Hebrews 2:13 and see Jesus as the suffering Saviour. As he thinks of Isaiah waiting for the LORD, who is hiding his face from the house of Jacob, Jesus sees himself wholly identified with God's rebellious children. In their place he will be thrust into deep darkness and suffer the gloom that Isaiah predicts (Isa. 8:22).

Then, on the cusp of this torment, holding the cup that will not pass from him, Jesus says, 'I will put my trust in Him.' The harder the trial, the stronger his faith—so strong that he goes on to say, 'Here am I, and the children God has given me.' Given the miserable state of the children and what he will have to suffer to make them perfect, he might reasonably refuse the gift. Yet he says, 'I will put my trust in him' to bring me through this darkness, to give me glory upon glory, and to make these children so perfect by what I am about to suffer that I will never want to let them go: 'Here am I, and the children God has given me.'

Continuing chronologically, in verse 12 we see Jesus the moment after he gave up his spirit. 'As he lands upon the shore, from that tempest wherein he was tossed in his passion, he cries out, "I will declare thy name unto my brethren...!"'[1] We now see Jesus in paradise, declaring to the Father what he will do when he rises again: 'I will declare your name.' To make sense of this we must recall how Psalm 22 begins, remembering that Jesus took ownership of the whole Psalm when he cried out, 'My God, my God, why have you forsaken me?' (v. 1). He was the man, scorned (v. 6), mocked, and despised (v. 7). He trusted in God from his birth (v. 9), but even though he cries, 'Be not far from me' (v. 11), he is laid in the dust of death (v. 15). He pleads, 'O LORD, do not be far off' (v. 19), when the LORD is incomprehensibly distant. But it is as if in his final anguished hours Jesus only got as far as verse 21 before he bowed his head. So now in paradise, he picks up where he left off, saying, 'I will declare your name to my brothers' (v. 22). His great desire now is to return for a while to stand among his friends and tell them that his cries have been heard: 'You who fear the LORD, praise him! ...for he has not despised or abhorred the affliction of the afflicted' (v. 24).

So that is what he does, not only claiming for himself the kingly authority, which the last verses of Psalm 22 ascribe to the Messiah, but sending his disciples out into the world to proclaim it to all nations. Not that his proclamation ends when the disciples see him taken up into heaven. 'In the midst of the assembly,' he says, 'I will sing praise to you.' Hebrews 12:23 identifies which assembly: 'to the general assembly and church

1 John Owen, *Exposition of the Epistle to the Hebrews* (London: Thomas Tegg, 1840), 377.

of the firstborn who are registered in heaven, to God the Judge of all, and to the spirits of just men made perfect.' That is where Jesus, the mediator of the new covenant, now sings praise. He is the object of praise, yet as a man in heaven, he is full of praise—praise to his God for his deliverance from death and for leading many sons to glory. As he praises he carries thousands upon thousands with him, uniting the church militant and the church triumphant in one song of praise.

The church below is full of people who often feel themselves to have more in common with the Jesus who owned the first part of Psalm 22 in his passion, as if they cry by day, but he does not answer, by night, but they find no rest. To them, Jesus proclaims the name of the LORD. He bids them see the love and kindness of his Father now made manifest in his glorified perfection, thereby assuring them that he will give them all the perfection they need, when one day they will see all things put under his feet: 'The meek shall eat and be satisfied' (Ps. 22:26). It must be so, for if the abyssal 'whatever' of Psalm 8:8 suggests 'Leviathan (cf. Ps. 104:26), the dreaded dragon,'[2] then our forerunner's perfection is also a proclamation of that beast's destruction: Christ 'has destroyed him that had the power of death, that is the devil' (Heb. 2:14). The church above certainly sees Satan's destruction more clearly than the church below. Thanatophobia—fear of death—never troubles them. Yet even they 'do not yet see' all things put under Christ's feet (Heb. 2:8). Though there be no dissatisfaction in the Jerusalem above, their satisfaction is yet incomplete, since without us 'they will not be made perfect' (Heb. 11:40). Our king does not lead two very different congregations in worship, only one. He unites us in praise and also in trust. Together, we trust him to take us by the hand and lead us in songs of praise that will delight our Father.

2 Waltke & Houston, *Psalms*, 271.

6

Return, O My Soul, to Your Rest

Psalm 116

Who would say such a thing?—'I love the LORD.' Can anyone speak like this? It seems so. This is everyday Christian speech: 'He loves the LORD.' 'She loves Christ.' 'I love Jesus.' It sounds like the familiar language of hymnody: 'Oh how I love Jesus…' 'My Jesus I love thee…' 'I'm so glad that I love Jesus…'

The saints of Scripture, however, are more timid. Which of them spoke with such confidence? In Psalm 18 David sings, 'I love you, O LORD, my strength,' but his is a lonely voice. At a stretch, we might think of Peter accompanying him, when Jesus asks him three times, 'Do you love me?' Peter replies—grieved—'You know that I love you' (John 21:15–17). Even Psalm 116's psalmist seems cautious. Isaac Leeser, the ninteenth century translator of an Old Testament 'for his fellow-Israelites' presents the opening words as 'It is lovely to me,' which may not have surprised anyone familiar with *The Book of Common Prayer*, which renders it: 'I am well

[1] I love because the LORD heard my voice of supplications.
[2] Because he inclined his ear to me,
all my days I will call on him.

[3] The cords of death encompassed me
and the straits of Sheol laid hold of me;
I found distress and sorrow.
[4] I called on the name of the LORD,
'Now LORD, rescue my soul.'
[5] The LORD is gracious and righteous;
our God is merciful.
[6] The LORD keeps the simple;
I was brought low and he saved me.
[7] Return my soul to your rest
for the LORD has dealt bountifully with you.
[8] For you delivered my soul from death,
my eyes from tears,
my feet from stumbling.

[9] I will walk before the LORD in the land of the living.
[10] I believed for I spoke,
'I am greatly afflicted.'
[11] I said in my alarm,
'All men are liars.'
[12] What shall I return to the LORD for all his benefits to me?
[13] I will lift up the cup of salvation
and call on the name of the LORD.
[14] I will complete my vows to the LORD before all his people.
[15] Precious in the eyes of the LORD is the death of his saints.
[16] Now LORD, I am your servant,
your servant, the son of your maidservant.
You have loosed my fetters.

[17] I will offer a sacrifice of thanksgiving to you
and call on the name of the LORD.
[18] I will pay my vows to the LORD before all his people,
[19] in the courts of the house of the LORD,
in your midst O Jerusalem.

Praise the LORD.

pleased.' Whatever the merits of those translations, they at least highlight that Psalm 116 is no brash declaration of love for God. A wooden translation could be, 'I love … because the LORD heard.' We assume the LORD is the object of his love, but he does not say it plainly.

Why such caution? Perhaps because this is not about how he feels, but about how he acts. If he says, 'I love the LORD,' is that not a claim to perfection? 'I love the LORD; I have no sin; I have fulfilled the law. I know the first and great commandment, "You shall love the LORD your God, with all your heart, with all your soul, and with all you might." And I have done exactly that. I love the LORD.'

That would be an audacious claim. The commandment to love the LORD is unexceptional; fulfilment of the commandment is beyond exceptional. Is it any wonder Scripture's saints say so rarely, 'I love the LORD'? Assuming that is how we should understand the psalmist's words, how can he say this? Does he imagine he loves the LORD as the commandment requires? He would hardly claim to love the LORD in a way that contradicts his commandment. So, yes, he does claim to fulfil the law, perhaps not with immediate and perfect obedience, but fully expecting such obedience. He says, 'I love the LORD,' confident that the penalty of the law will not apply to him. He speaks as if he were a perfect man. The whole psalm tells us how he can do that, but the first two verses sum it up. His love for the LORD does not spring from an innate ability to obey the law. Though the law commands him to love, it gives him no power. He loves the LORD because the LORD heard his cries, stooped down to listen, and rescued him. That rescue empowered him to love the LORD and set him on course of life-long loving. To put it another way, he loves because God first loved him.

Singing Psalm 116 means taking possession of this bold claim, 'I love the LORD.' Psalms 113–115, with their call to united praise, might have allowed nominal worshippers to grab a free ride; Psalm 116 shakes off religious parasites. Its switch from 'we' to 'I' and from 'us' to 'me' declares that God's saving work in the Exodus must be realized in every life. In some ways, Psalm 116 personalizes aspects of Psalm 113. Psalm 118 will do the same with Psalm 115. Yet Psalm 116 is not a solo. When we sing, 'I love the LORD,' we identify not just with one another, but with someone.

Long ago, that might have been David, or King Hezekiah, a psalmist whose words take us on a mini-Exodus—a personal flight from groaning in bondage to willing service before the LORD. That does not mean the psalmist is just beginning with God. The exodus was not Israel's first encounter with God and nor is this the psalmist's. He already knows God. Psalm 116 contains at least one chapter from his autobiography, perhaps even a repeating chapter that tells of a long night in Doubting Castle. Yet his back is never toward Zion. He is in the way, facing the city, looking to recover a foretaste of its blessings, so that he can say to himself, 'Return, O my soul, to your rest' (v. 7). That is his immediate ambition.

Discussions about the structure of Psalm 116 often become complex, not least because the Greek Septuagint (second century BC) divided it into two Psalms, verses 1–9 (numbered Psalm 114) and verses 10–19 (numbered Psalm 115). Some interpreters like to adopt that 'traditional' twofold structure,[1] while others prefer more recent proposals for three, four, or even five parts.[2] Sifting through the arguments for those alternatives may prove more perplexing than rewarding, and the ancient twofold division at least has some convergence with the flow of the Psalm. At some point, whether at verse 10 or gradually, despair and pleading yield to deliverance and

1 For example, Michael L. Barré, 'Psalm 116: Its Structure and Its Enigmas.' *Journal of Biblical Literature* 109/1 (1990), 63.

2 See Leslie C. Allen, *Psalms 101–150*, WBC, 21 (Dallas: Word, 2002). 153.

thanksgiving. This chapter recognises that two-fold structure and change of mood as follows:

- Verses 3–8 recount the psalmist's experience. Simply put: 'I was brought low; he saved me' (v. 6).
- Verses 9–16 proclaim his hope for the future: 'I will walk before the LORD in the land of the living' (v. 9).

Verses 1–2 and 17–19 enclose those two halves, so that the last verses of the Psalm correspond to its opening. Someone who loves the LORD and calls on him all his days (vv. 1–2) offers thanksgiving and pays his vows to the LORD, not in isolation, but with God's people and in his house (vv. 17–19).

I Was Brought Low; He Saved Me

Where is the psalmist at the beginning of verses 3–8? Or perhaps better first to ask, where does he want to be? He longs for a place where all the benefits of Psalms 113–115 flow into his life. Hazy hopes for the future will not do. He wants the LORD to remember him, bless him, and give him life that will never end—now: 'Why should I only sing of God's power in an exodus past? Must I only reminisce about the water flowing from the rock? Give me the water. Let me taste God's saving power. Fill my mouth with praise.'

But all that is out of reach. No refreshment. No power. No blessing: 'The cords of death encompassed me, the anguish of Sheol laid hold of me' (v. 3). How perplexing: on the march with God's people, the old world left behind, blessing and life on the horizon, yet in hellish straits, under a weight of darkness that the brightest dawn will not shift. As with the short winter days and granite skies of a Nordic winter, Psalm 115's post-exodus blues pass. But not this. Like Jonah, buried alive in his submarine prison, certain death confronts the psalmist: 'The waters encompassed me even to my soul; the deep overwhelmed me...I went down to the earth whose bars closed behind me forever' (Jonah 2:5–6). No way back to life. Providence signs every escape route: 'NO EXODUS.'

Perhaps he needs counselling. Someone should tell him, 'Listen, your situation is awful, death inescapable, but the grave is not the end. You will be gathered to your fathers. You should even meet Enoch, who walked with God, and then he was not, for God took him. Things can only get better.'

That would be stupid counsel, of little help to someone who fears a double-death. Were dying his only concern, he could, like so many, just rage against the dying of the light, bargain his way from anger to depression, and then from acceptance to 'hope.'[3] But such rage is not for those who fear the LORD. They cannot afford the luxury of resignation, nor find succour in some forced affirmation that 'death is nothing at all'. So, he says, 'I found distress and sorrow' (v. 3). Something in him, some irrepressible conviction and unquenchable hope, demands this response—distress, grief, anguish. They have him in their grip, constricted and confined, beyond therapy, and every human solution.

Why? Why blackness so unassailable? He believes that God exists, that he made heaven and earth, that he freed his people from bondage, that he raises the poor from the dust, and that apart from God there is no life. But where is the psalmist? Apart from God. He does not expect to open his eyes in glory. Not for him the blessing and the life of those who trust in the LORD; death drags him down into the silent land of the twice-dead, who trusted in dumb idols. Why would someone who knows God find themselves in such bondage, in a place that seems to be even worse than the place they began?

3 Elisabeth Kübler Ross, *On Death and Dying* (London: Tavistock Publications, 1970), 122–138.

Two passages, which Psalm 116 may echo, Psalm 18 and Isaiah 38, present us with the most likely cause. In Isaiah 38 we find Hezekiah, a king about to die without an heir. In Psalm 18, we meet David, an anointed king, yet hunted for his life. Two kings, expecting the LORD to keep his promise that David's throne would be forever; two kings, in circumstances where they felt his promise could fail. And they both say much the same thing, 'The cords of death encompassed me' (Ps. 18:4); death and the grave had a grip on me. Yet the thought of their own dying does not disturb them so much as the thought that their deaths would spell the death of the LORD's promise. And if the LORD would not keep his promise to David, what promise would he keep? If David and his sons lose the throne, all is lost, every promise void. Death and hell have the victory. That's the blackness in Psalm 116. It is here in the psalms, for God's children when they think of God's mighty work, of an Exodus from Egypt, or of Christ's greater Exodus, yet fear that for themselves, all is lost.

This is not usual anti-climax or corporate dispiritedness, but deep, private despair. And the saints are not immune. Indeed, someone who doubts God, or who questions Christ's power to save, can know nothing of this blackness. It emerges not from the sceptic's question, 'Can he save?' but from the believer's question, 'Will he save me?' 'There is salvation with him, but not for me; forgiveness with him, but not for me; blessing with him, but not for me; life with him, but not for me.'

How does this anxiety possess a Christian believer, who, after all, is not a king in the line of David upon whose future the future of God's people depends? Is sin the problem? Some think Psalm 116 the testimony of someone suffering the consequences of specific sin, as in several other psalms. No doubt, such a person who persists in sin—public or private—or who pursues a lifestyle they ought to flee, will become despondent. If someone can set their heart on a disobedient course, yet not become troubled or distressed, whatever way they are going, it is not heavenward.

Specific sin, however, is not the direct cause of the psalmist's sorrow, and no Christian believer is a king of Israel. Even so, the spiritual dynamics are the same. I go through life as a Christian, seeking to hold onto God's promises, but then trouble comes—small or great, at work or at home, touching health, wealth, or family. I pray and I hope, but the troubles increase. I try to rest in God's promises, but anxiety overwhelms trust. I have no peace, so I think I have no faith. And if I have no faith in small matters, surely I have no faith in great matters:

'I believe the Gospels—Christ died to save his people from their sins, but is that not meant to transform my life? The New Testament speaks of peace that passes understanding, of inexpressible and glorious joy, but what do I know about that? God ignores my prayers. He is not fulfilling his promises for me in this life, so I have no hope for the next life.'

So, why do despondent Christians not get up and say, 'Well, if God will not go on with me, I will just go on without him'? We cannot do that. The cords of death entangle, grief and sorrow overwhelm, and we cannot escape, not because we have no faith, but because we have faith.

Unbelief is easy. Trust in dead idols is as undemanding as it is stupid. Faith in the unseen God is hard; when you lay hold of him by faith, he lays hold of you, and puts your faith to the test to prove it genuine. Out of grief and sorrow, out of unassailable blackness, he produces saints, more sure of what they hope for and more certain of what they do not see. They began with the LORD, and they may not understand why he had to take them on this route, but they say with Hezekiah that it was for my peace, or welfare, 'that I suffered such bitterness' (Isa. 38:17).

But how do I leave the blackness behind? Only one way; keep exercising faith in the unseen God: 'Then I called on the name of the LORD: "O LORD, deliver my soul!"' (v. 4). The psalmist need not force this plea. Neither deep distress nor prolonged darkness can silence him. This is the one thing he cannot resist doing. Faith conquers hopelessness with a single cry, 'O LORD, deliver my soul!' As in Psalms 113 and 115, 'the name of the LORD' sums up the sort of salvation he seeks: 'Deliver me according to your character, on your terms, not mine.'

In verse 5 he spells it out; he truly seeks a mini-exodus: 'The LORD is gracious and righteous; our God is merciful.' That's the God who proclaimed his name to Moses, 'the LORD, the LORD,' who took Israel out of Egypt. 'All the grace and compassion he showed to our fathers when they groaned in Egypt, he will show it to me now. He promised them, "I will bring you to a land…flowing with milk and honey," and he did what he promised because he is righteous. And he is righteous still, so he will fulfil his promises for me. All the power and wisdom he displayed in the Exodus, he will put into service for my salvation. He will hold nothing back to disentangle me from the cords of death.'

Should someone say, 'You are so naïve—too simple,' he will reply, 'Good. I want to be simple because the LORD preserves the simple' (v. 6). Is that good? Sometimes in the Old Testament, to be simple is not good—the opposite of being wise—but this is about uncomplicated trust in the LORD. He may deal with us in a perplexing and mysterious way, but we neither hedge our bets, nor try to answer questions that are beyond us. It is enough to say, 'Yes, I am simple. Some people would say, childish. But did not Jesus say that his Father reveals the most important matters to such people? (Matt. 11:25). And in response, even he was simple—childlike: "Even so, Father, for this was your good pleasure"' (Matt. 11:26).

In deep darkness and sorrow, I want to be like that. If my progress with the LORD includes a disruption that feels like hell, even then I want to have simple-hearted, child-like faith, which says, 'Even so, Father, for this was your good pleasure.' In fact, having such faith is a matter of life and death because the LORD preserves the simple. That was this psalmist's experience: 'I was brought low, I was in great need, he saved me' (v. 6).

Verse 8 sums up the outcome: the LORD delivers him from death—the double-death of physical destruction and spiritual disaster. The LORD wipes every tear from his eyes; no more sorrow and distress. And the LORD kept him from stumbling; even when he was in the crucible, his faith tested to breaking point, the LORD did not allow him to fall. That is how the LORD answers when one of his children cries out, 'Deliver, my soul.'

The psalmist says to himself, 'Take hold of that deliverance. Lay hold on the blessings of the destination. "Return, O my soul, to your rest" (v. 7). That exodus from Egypt, this is what it was all about—bringing God's people to a land of rest and a place of security, to be at home with the LORD, and to praise him, free from every hindrance and handicap. Take a hold of it: "Return, O my soul, to your rest."'

Yet following his example may seem impossible, so that someone responds, 'But I cannot return to my rest. I am still in distress. My lap is full of trouble. I barely have the strength to cry, "O LORD, deliver, my soul."'

Where can you go then? How about going back to the Upper Room and to the Last Passover? Remember that when we sing, 'I love the LORD,' we identify with someone, who for us is not Hezekiah or David, but their greatest son. Psalm 116 became our Lord's harrowing testimony as the griefs and sorrows of all God's children converged upon him. This Psalm can only be true for me if it was true for him. I can only sing, 'I love the LORD,' if I sing it with him and because of him.

So return to the eve of his Passion and hear our Lord Jesus sing with his disciples: 'I love the LORD…' And he does—as no other man loved the LORD, with all his heart and soul and might. 'He heard my voice…' And he did—thundering from heaven in response to Jesus' prayers (John 12:28).

It might be enough for Jesus to stop there, but he sings on: 'The pains of hell took hold on me, I grief and trouble found.' He has had sorrow enough already, a heart so troubled that he cried out, 'Father, save me from this hour.' But that was little compared to the trouble to come and to what he is about to suffer. Countless believers before him, and after him, felt the death-pangs and anguish of verse 3. Some of them may have traced their trouble to specific sin, while many others simply could not reconcile the LORD's promises with their experience. Will his death void the LORD's covenant? Will he see corruption? Will his tomb memorialise hell's victory? These are not theoretical questions for Jesus; tomorrow, all theorizing ends. He will put the promise under unprecedented and unrepeatable stress as he identifies with every sinful and despairing believer. He will embrace trouble and sorrow such as they have never known and from which they deserved no release. As he does so, the cords of death will not so much take a hold of him as he will take a hold of them, and break their power forever.

So, how can I say, 'I cannot return to my rest, I cannot lay hold on the blessings'? Will I think so little of his anguish that I hesitate to say, 'Return, O my soul to your rest'? What right do I have to refuse to sing with this Jesus Christ, and so to identify with him, who identified with me in all my sin and need, taking all my trouble and sorrow on his sacred head? In him all the anguish and pain of God's people is resolved. From him flows all life and blessing. 'Return, O my soul to your rest.'

I Will Walk Before the Lord in the Land of the Living

If Psalm 116 contains at least one chapter from the psalmist's biography, perhaps verse 9 marks either a final paragraph, or the beginning of a new chapter. Either way, it signals a change of mood as the final destination of verse 19 comes into sharper focus. What does he need after the crisis? Not respite and recuperation. Though he said to his soul, 'Return to your rest,' that is not because the LORD will put him to sleep. This rest animates: 'I can get up and go—I will walk before the LORD in the land of the living.' That may sound demanding, but the LORD's deliverance saves completely. Hesitation in the name of recuperation is no return to rest, but unbelief that risks the recovery: 'He freed my feet from stumbling, not so I might put them up, but so that I would get going. This is my mini-exodus. A part of Israel is on the march in me.' For all Israel, the 'land of the living' will be journey's end, yet every sojourner lays hold on its blessings ahead of time, because its life already has a hold of them, drawing them to a house not made with hands. That is how they get the strength to walk 'before the LORD.'

None of this means that the psalmist is in denial. He will not pretend that the 'pains of hell' were the mere phantasmagoria of a nightmare. His scars speak to him of a real ordeal and of a true deliverance. Though he is no longer traumatised, yesterday's paralysing trauma stimulates him today, so that he is unafraid to recall the period when he said in his alarm—'I am greatly afflicted' (v. 10); 'All men are liars' (v. 11). Now that the blackness has cleared, he sees that a hopeless man would never have spoken like that: 'I believed, *therefore* I spoke.' Silence and dumbness is for hopeless people; faith cries out, even protests, against unbelief. In retrospect, 'hopeless' lament turns out to be faith-saturated affirmation of covenant love and faithfulness. Perhaps he understood that even in his alarm. Why would he have said, 'All men are liars,' if not because he knew that a lie underpins every mocking question (as in Psalm 115:2)? Whether the 'liar' was someone beside him saying that his faith rested on a phantom God, or a voice inside him making the diabolic suggestion that his faithlessness would nullify God's faithfulness, either way, like the psalmist in Psalm 51:4 and the apostle after him (Rom. 3:3–4), his faith in the truthfulness of God constrains him to say, 'All men are liars.'

How much faith does someone need to defy universal opinion, to declare, *contra mundum*, 'All men are liars,' and to cling to their God for deliverance? That is, doubtless, a ridiculous question; a mustard-seed's worth could turn the world upside down. How much faith is not the issue, but what kind of faith. Quoting Psalm 116:10 in 2 Corinthians 4, Paul writes we have the 'same spirit of faith…knowing that he who raised the Lord Jesus, shall also raise us with Jesus…' (vv. 13–14). That was the psalmist's kind of faith, and the kind of faith our Lord Jesus exemplified when he sang Psalm 116. It is also the faith God gifts to us, so we believe that the LORD who freed Israel from Egypt has liberated us from a greater captivity, through a Saviour who was brought low to break the cords of death, that we may say with firm assurance, 'I will walk before the LORD in the land of the living.' Yet again, just one cry, 'O LORD, deliver my soul!' will carry you all the way to the resurrection morning and the new creation.

What can I give to the LORD in return for that? (v. 12). What will I give? What is it worth to me? I could ask the LORD, 'What do you want me to give?' And this is what he will do. He will hand me a cup, and say, 'Drink.' That is the cup of salvation (v. 13a). Whoever wants to give something to the LORD, must do this: take. Take, and take again. Lift up the cup. Take the salvation he offers.

What a paradox for proud men and women: the greatest and the only thing I can give to the LORD is to become a wholly dependent receiver. When the psalmist did that, everything else followed—a life of prayerful reliance on the LORD and his covenant love (v. 13b), matched by a public commitment to his Redeemer. He unbound the cords of death that held me fast, so I bind myself to him: 'Now LORD, I am your servant' (v. 16). In communion with my fellow redeemed, I express my pledge in thanksgiving, worship, and service (vv. 14, 17–19).

Whoever takes that route belongs to those of whom the psalmist says, 'Precious [or costly] in the eyes of the LORD, is the death of his saints' (v. 15). Why precious? Perhaps Paul also answers that in 2 Corinthians 4 when he describes the trials of an apostle: 'We are hard pressed on every side, yet not crushed; we are perplexed, but not in despair; persecuted, but not forsaken; struck down, but not destroyed' (vv. 8–9). In verse 13 he will quote Psalm 116:10, but his quotation recalls 'the entire story of Psalms 114–115 LXX [i.e. Psalm 116]…because, according to the apostle, *these psalms tell the story of Jesus.*'[4] Indeed the whole Psalm may still be on his mind in the first verses of 2 Corinthians 5, as if he says, 'The psalmist puts our experience into song. He was always carrying the dying of a coming Jesus; we of a crucified Jesus. We were always carrying in the body the dying of Jesus, so that the life of Jesus may also be manifested in our bodies. In all our pain, in all our anxiety and bewilderment about the churches, trying to reconcile God's promise with our experience, in all our Christ-like dying, the life of Jesus was flowing through us into the church and into your lives.' Without the death and dying there is no life and living. From the first believer's first entanglement with death on to the last believer's final encounter with death, in all their blackness and bewilderment, God makes his children bearers of the life of his Son. Is anything more precious to God?

Nothing is more precious, yet we could still ask, how precious? How precious is the death of a saint in the eyes of the LORD? So precious that he refuses to lose even one of them

4 Thomas D. Stegman, ' Ἐπὶστευσα, διὸἐλάλησα (2 Corinthians 4:13): Paul's Christological Reading of Psalm 115: 1a LXX in *Catholic Biblical Quarterly* 69 (2007), 732.

in the process. And how costly will that refusal be for him? So costly that he will require the most precious life of Jesus to guarantee that not one saint will be given over to death. It is this unreckonable cost, and the manner of its payment, that makes the experience of Psalm 116 an inextricable component in the life of every servant of God.

Discussions about 2 Corinthians 4:13 and its reference to Psalm 116 often quote Richard Hays' phrase "christological ventriloquism",[5] as though Paul were a great ventriloquist who makes his Messiah sing David's songs. But if Paul thought of himself as a ventriloquist, he would judge himself of all men most miserable. There is no ventriloquism in his christology. His Christ sings as he suffers, and because he suffered. Nor is there any ventriloquism in the apostle's doctrine of the Christian life. He does not speak of 'the dying of Jesus' because Christians must make some small imitation of the sufferings of their dying Lord. Imitation is inadequate; this is more than acting. Christ calls his servants into a living connection with his affliction and perplexity. They must proclaim his suffering and dying, not in word only, but in weakness and apparent failure, and not for a moment only, but always. The psalmist proclaimed it in advance; we proclaim it thereafter. Every child of God must carry this burden. To put it down is to put Christ down. The life of Jesus does not flow to others through the lives of unperplexed ministers or unbroken Christians. The weight of their dying corresponds to the fullness of life and treasure that flows through them to others.

This too is a paradox. No one wants to endlessly relive the horror of verse 3, or even to return for a day trip. Better to

5 Richard D. Hays, 'Christ Prays the Psalms: Paul's Use of an Early Christian Exegetical Convention', in Abraham J. Malherbe and Wayne A. Meeks (eds.), *The Future of Christology: Essays in Honor of Leander E. Keck* (Minneapolis: Fortress Press, 1993), 104. Also, Stegman, ''Επὶστευσα, διὸἐλάλησα', 726; Scott, *Hermeneutics of Christological Psalmody*, 138.

'rest' in verse 7. Even so, the horror and the agony has a strange attraction, not because faith has a masochistic streak, but because we long for the rest, the life, and the love of Psalm 116 more than we fear its horrors. We know that rest, life, and love flourish most in those who die most, and even endure a cross for the sake of joy ahead. We see the life-producing pattern as we observe his saints' death, and perhaps even in ourselves.

Knowing this now does not mean that should the LORD call you back into verse 3, all will make perfect sense. The unsurpassed wisdom of our Lord Jesus did not mean he could sing those words without perplexity. So how could he, and how shall we, embrace the mystery of Psalm 116 and speak such paradox? Only by 'the same spirit of faith.' With apostles and psalmists, with Jesus as our leader, we believe and therefore we speak, saying, 'Deliver my soul!…Return, O my soul, to your rest.…You have loosed my bonds.' Fully identified with the maidservant's son (v. 16), we will even say, 'I love the LORD.'

If this is a mystery, it is one that brings you to your destination and to your final resting place. Not some sodden grave, but the house of the LORD, in the midst of Jerusalem (v. 19). There, incomparable glory supplants momentary affliction (2 Cor. 4:18) and life swallows up mortality (2 Cor. 5:4).

'Hallelujah!' (v. 19).

7

Follow the Conductor

Psalm 117

On April 14 2013, Sir Colin Davis died at the age of eighty-five. He was a grand old man of the classical music world and conductor of the London Symphony Orchestra until he retired in 2006. In an hour-long portrait of his life, shown on BBC4 shortly before his death, Sir Colin spoke about life, death, and religion. The interviewer asked, 'Are you a religious man?' In a response, full of long pauses, Sir Colin said,

> ...I don't know...I don't go to church and...but I am deeply moved by the great religious music that we have. It's very interesting isn't it that the great romantic religious music is all about the requiem and the last great mass was Beethoven's D Major mass...and when I'm doing those pieces I really...I do believe in the whole thing...

Next we see Sir Colin conducting the *Gloria* from that work, and you would think, 'Yes, he really does believe in the whole

[1] Praise the LORD all nations.
Magnify him all peoples.
[2] For great is his loving-kindness towards us.
And the faithfulness of the LORD never fails.
Praise the LORD.

thing.' He conducts orchestra and choir with such passion and conviction that it seems his whole being is saying,

Glory to God in the highest…
we praise you,
we bless you,
we worship you,
we glorify you…
O Lord God, Heavenly King…

The whole performance could well be some splendid confession of his own faith. But the music stops. The applause fades. And Sir Colin, no more deeply moved, says, 'I don't know.'

Not being part of the Mass ordinary, Psalm 117 did not appear in Beethoven's *Missa solemnis*, but as the fifth Psalm in Mozart's *Vesperae solennes de confessore*, it normally finds a place in lists with titles like *100 Ultimate Classical Music Masterpieces.* How many of those who love listening to *Laudate dominum* know they are hearing the words of Psalm 117? Perhaps only a small minority, whose love of the music likewise does not indicate that they believe the whole thing.

Down through the centuries, churchgoers in many traditions have known Psalm 117 as part of their liturgy. Their musical performances probably did not match the London Symphony Orchestra and Chorus, but the greatest challenge in singing Psalm 117 has always been spiritual and intellectual rather than musical. To sing the words of this psalm and to really believe the whole thing requires great conviction. For it to be of any worth, we need a conductor—someone to direct our worship, who is not only deeply moved, but who truly believes. It is no use if he descends the podium only to say, 'I don't know.'

One may look at this psalm and think there is not much to it—anyone can sing, 'Praise the LORD, all you nations.' Not so. Psalm 117 is a revolutionary and counter-cultural hymn. Why?

'Praise the LORD'—nothing new in that; the previous four psalms said the same thing. Yes, but they did not say, 'Praise the LORD, all nations.' Psalm 113 called on the servants of the LORD to praise the LORD. Psalm 114 called on the earth to tremble at the presence of the LORD. Psalm 115 has nothing to say to the nations. No point in asking the nations to praise the LORD; they are the twice dead—spiritually dead worshippers of dumb idols, who face a second death, as they go down into the silence of verse 17, where no one praises the LORD. Psalm 116, likewise, has nothing to say to the nations.

But now this, in Psalm 117: 'Praise the LORD, all nations.' On the face of it, that is completely stupid. Why would the nations praise Israel's God? And why would the people of God call on the nations to praise their LORD? He had not saved the nations, but driven them out. Out of all the nations, he chose Israel. Why should the nations praise the LORD? How can they praise the LORD? These diehard sons of Adam are as stupid and blind as their idols, hostile to God, and in rebellion against him. God has not revealed himself to them, but left them in darkness. They cannot praise the LORD.

To call on them to praise the LORD is not only out of place, but highly controversial. Psalm 117 would be (or should be) an incendiary anthem at a multi-faith service. To sing this psalm, is to call upon all nations to turn from their gods, and to praise the LORD. 'Praise the LORD all nations: our God demands your allegiance.' These opening words are not obvious or safe. They call on the nations to do something revolutionary and even impossible, something they may find offensive.

So to sing this psalm, we need conviction. Specifically, we need to be sure that somehow people of all nations will have cause and ability to praise the LORD. We need conviction that makes us willing to take up the call of Psalm 117, whatever the cost. Most of all, we need someone to conduct our worship and lead us in our praise, whose belief will not fade with the music.

Given the Psalm's brevity, any outline risks being longer than the text, so in the following pages I will aim to answer two questions about Psalm 117. First, who speaks? Or more precisely, who presides over our worship? The second question is, what is his message? Why does he think that all nations should praise the LORD?

The Singer

The question, 'Who speaks?' is not the same as the question, 'Who wrote this?' Someone could write something intended for someone else to speak. Sometimes it helps to know who wrote a Psalm, but the psalter often likes to respect the anonymity of its poets, leaving the author's identity a matter of speculation. Perhaps that is because it may be more important to know who the Psalms were written for. Who had to take ownership of these songs? Who becomes the speaker?

Earlier in this book (p. 30), I mentioned Lefebvre's account of 1 Chronicles 25 as a description of King David's 'hymnwriting workshops'. His second chapter,[1] provides part of the answer to the question, 'Who speaks?' 1 Chronicles 25 teaches us something about how the Psalms came together. By the time some readers have reached Gedaliah, Zeri, Jeshaiah, Shimei, Hashabiah, and Mattithiah in verse 3, they might conclude the sooner they can move on to something more interesting the better. But in this ancient Directory of Musicians, there are some names that should be familiar to readers of Scripture because they also appear in the titles of various Psalms—names like Asaph, Heman, or Jeduthun. The first person we meet should certainly be no stranger: King David (v. 1), not for the moment occupied with the affairs of state, or fighting wars, but busy organising something that will outlast any state and

1 Lefebvre, *Singing the Songs of Jesus*, 31–56.

its institutions. David sets apart the sons of Asaph, Heman, and Jeduthun—288 trained singers, in twenty-four groups of twelve, best seen in Lefebvre's organizational chart.[2] Their task was to 'prophesy' (v. 1, 2, 3), not simply as foretellers, but as proclaimers of the words of God, and in crafting words fit for worship. They composed songs and psalms, which were gathered together, and which became part of our 150 Psalms. Chronicles insists that all this work went on under the king's guidance (vv. 2, 6). David sets out to produce a songbook fit for a king—for himself and for his sons. That does not mean it was to be a private royal collection; this is a songbook for a nation, for a people under God, designed to bring them as one—a people and their king—into the presence of the LORD.

David's songs will never be like the British national anthem, where the congregation sings, but only the monarch stays silent; David and his sons sing. The king conducts worship and leads the congregation in song. A few chapters later, we read of David blessing the LORD in the presence of all the assembly (1 Chron. 29:10), before instructing them to follow his example (v. 20). After David's death, Solomon built the temple, and like his father, he led the assembly in worship and praise (2 Chron. 6–7). Kings come and go, some good, some evil. Some, like Ahaz, cast aside the law of God; they lead the people into death and idolatry, not into the presence of the LORD. Others, like Hezekiah, Ahaz' son, seek the LORD. He restored the temple that his father plundered and gathered the assembly to worship (2 Chron. 29), commanding the Levites to praise the LORD with the words that David and Asaph had composed (v. 30). Hezekiah's great grandson, Josiah, likewise led the people back to the LORD after years of apostasy. 2 Chronicles 35 prints the full report. He restored the Passover, and even then, sixteen generations after David, the singers, Asaph's sons, took their

2 Ibid, 35.

places according to the command of David, Asaph, Heman, and Jeduthun (2 Chron. 35:15)—familiar names.

It should have been like that generation after generation, king after king leading the LORD's people to a higher throne, and showing them what it meant to praise the LORD. But there were few Hezekiahs and Josiahs. King after king did what was evil. They did not even rise so high as to direct the people in worship, only to say at the end of it, 'I don't know.' These useless, corrupt, evil worship-leaders only led the people into idolatry and brought them under judgment. Even the best of them, the Hezekiahs and Josiahs, were less than perfect. Israel never had a king that was fully up to the job of conducting them into the LORD's presence. No king led their praises with such conviction as would never fade away. But when true prophets write your songs, they will give you songs for exactly that situation. David and his 288 hymnists bequeathed to them laments for a nation under judgment and plaintive cries for a people longing for release. We find several of these between Psalm 73 and Psalm 89. They also had psalms like Psalm 72, full of hope and expectancy that their king would reign from shore to shore, saving the needy, and bringing blessing to all nations.

But what king of Israel had such a glorious reign? Not David, not Hezekiah, not Josiah, not even dazzling Solomon. The best king, leading the most sanctified people in the heartiest praise, could not match those expectations or bring them to fulfilment. We do not know when exactly Psalms 113–118 came to be in the Psalter, but here they are as part of this songbook, designed for a king to lead his people heavenward. It is easy to see how David and his sons could sing Psalms 113 to 115 with the people; it was their shared history. We can imagine how they could own Psalm 116, which echoes David's words in Psalm 18, and Hezekiah's words in Isaiah 38—two kings of Israel, for whom personal salvation was also Israel's salvation. But what about Psalm 117: 'Praise the LORD all nations'?

'Really David? Really Solomon? Really Josiah? You have been remarkable kings, but do you really believe this whole thing? More to the point, how do you expect us to believe this whole thing? Your royal sons and ancestors have hardly been national king material, far less kings before whom all other kings must bow. If you want us to join in this song with you, please forgive us if we only lip-synch.'

That leaves us in a situation, where by this point, we can give half an answer to the first question, 'Who speaks?' Who are the words of Psalm 117 for? As with every Psalm, they are for the king, for David and his sons. They are words from God, with which they can go to God, and lead the people into his presence.

Yet this problem remains: David and his sons were not up to the job. Their conviction rarely endured a generation. Those psalms were too good for Israel and her kings. So how could they sing them? How could God's people do that, especially in a time after the exile, when they had no king? Perhaps they could sing because, like Beethoven's quartets, they knew them to be songs 'for a later age' (see p. 33). They do not belong to a past age. Psalm 117 is too grand and too good, too demanding and too extensive—much too big for any king of Israel and his assembly. This is a song for a later age. Yet as one of this collection of Passover hymns, Psalm 117 also became one of the last songs of an earlier age as Jesus sang it with his disciples before he laid himself on the altar. What were they thinking as they sang this with him? Perhaps they hoped he would be another Josiah—a king who would lead assembled Israel's Passover celebrations. Even after the resurrection, before Pentecost came, they thought Jesus would be that sort of king. But what sort of king did Jesus expect to be?

When Jesus sings Psalm 117 at that last Passover, he takes complete ownership of these words. If they were written for any son of David, they were written for him. He will sing with enduring belief. The Spirit of the Lord rests upon this anointed king in such measure that he will conduct our worship with conviction, which transports us with him into the presence of the LORD. How does he do that? He becomes, in Paul's words, 'a minister, or a servant, of the circumcision' (Rom. 15:8). The eternal Son of God makes himself low. He does not please himself, but bears the reproach that falls upon God's people (Rom. 15:3). When in verse 3, Paul quotes Psalm 69, he wants us to know that in one way or another, all the words of Psalm 69 became Christ's words.

To illustrate how such citations of the Old Testament in the New Testament work, imagine being in a group of people as a magnificent bore wearies everyone with an account of his appreciating property and marvellously successful investments. Eventually, someone who can take no more, interrupts, 'What shall it profit a man?' and storms off. At this point, if you only think, 'What a lunatic,' you probably do not know your Bible. If, on the other hand, you know your Bible, you may still judge the interrupter a lunatic, yet it all makes good sense. In your mind, you finish the quotation, 'What shall it profit a man if he shall gain the whole world and lose his own soul?' You get the point because you know the Scriptures.

Many New Testament quotations of the Old Testament work like that. You need to know the Old Testament, especially the Psalms, if you want to understand the New. So when we hear Paul quote Psalm 69:9 in Romans 15, we go back to Psalm 69, and ask, how have these words become Christ's words? Surely when the psalmist speaks of folly and guilt (Ps. 69:5), Christ had to fall silent? Not so. He still speaks, not because he was foolish or guilty, but because he became a 'servant of the circumcision.' He identifies voluntarily with God's people, even in their folly and guilt. In that he becomes a true king, the best son that David ever had. 'He has pity on the weak' (Ps. 72:14). He understands pain and confusion—the pain and confusion of believing, yet being in a position where every outward indicator seems to ridicule his belief. That is his position now as he sings with his disciples, 'Praise the LORD all nations.'

'Really Jesus? How are you going to make that happen? You think you are greater than Solomon? Why then are you about to die? Where is your glory? Your majesty? Your strength? Will all nations bow to you? Tell us that tomorrow, when the words you have just been singing from Psalm 116 become your experience. Tell us that when the cords of death entangle you and the pains of Hell take hold of you. Jesus of Nazareth, King of the Jews, you would save yourself so much trouble, if you would just have the humility to say, "I don't know."'

Except Jesus had a different sort of humility. His version of humility meant depending on God and believing his promises even when the waters have come up over his head and he is in freefall, sinking without a foothold. That is why he can sing Psalm 117 in faith—faith that will eventually carry him, and us with him, into the presence of the LORD forevermore. He sings with his disciples convinced that the LORD of Psalm 117 is also the God of Psalm 114. If mountains crumpled and seas shrank at the presence of the LORD, Jesus is persuaded that the LORD will also use what he is about to undergo to bring nations to praise the LORD and all peoples to magnify him.

Thank God that our Lord Jesus had such faith and conviction. Apart from that, the call of this psalm would indeed be ridiculous. We who belong to 'the nations' would never praise the LORD. Romans 15:8–9 tells us that is what it was all about: Christ became a servant 'to confirm the promises given to the fathers…and so that the Gentiles might glorify God for his mercy.' Then immediately Paul quotes Psalm 18:49: 'As it is written: 'Therefore I will praise you among the Gentiles; I will sing to your name' (Rom. 15:9). That Psalm is something like a non-identical twin to Psalm 116, and the point is that though our king cried out, 'LORD, deliver my soul,' when entangled by death's snares, he now has the victory. He praises God among the Gentiles because the LORD delivered his soul from death. Christ lives, to proclaim: 'Rejoice, O Gentiles with his people' (Rom. 15:10).

But how does his 'hymn' go on? What does the risen Christ sing? Romans 15:11 gives the answer: 'Praise the Lord, all you nations [or Gentiles], and extol him all you peoples.' Psalm 117—the perfect song, for a risen, conquering, son of David, Son of God. The risen Christ conducts our worship, not just with the conviction of someone who holds onto God in the darkness, but with the conviction of someone whose faith in God has been vindicated. The only way to sing this impossible, counter-cultural hymn—'Praise the LORD all nations'—with confidence and with conviction is to sing with the risen, ascended Christ.

His Song

Beyond the call to praise the LORD, what is the message of Psalm 117? What does Christ say to us? What do we say with him when we take up the words of the psalm? Here it is: 'For his lovingkindness is great towards us, and the truth [or faithfulness] of the LORD endures for ever' (v. 2). The first verse of Psalm 115 also proclaimed the LORD's love and faithfulness. Merciful kindness, or steadfast love, sums up all that his name represents; when he loves, he invests all his qualities and powers in loving his people. His faithfulness sums up the way he kept loving his people, and kept fulfilling his promises, even when they stopped loving him. Psalm 117 makes some small additions to Psalm 115's proclamation of his love and faithfulness.

First, his love is 'great,' which does not just mean 'big,' or 'wonderful'. This is the language of victory and complete success—total conquest. When the LORD binds himself in covenant love to any people, nothing in heaven, or earth, or hell, can obstruct his love. It will break Egyptian chains, sink Pharaoh in the depths, and tear down the walls of Jericho.

Second, his faithfulness endures 'for ever'. It hardly seems necessary to say that. If faithfulness does not endure, ordinarily, that means it has become unfaithfulness. So why say it 'endures for ever'? God's people say it, because their faithfulness has so often become unfaithfulness. They gave the LORD no end of grounds for divorce. Justly, he might have abandoned them in the wilderness, left them to the Philistines, or deserted them in Babylon. But his fidelity overcomes all their infidelity. Generations of Israelites remembered that Passover after Passover.

It would be easy to assume that when Christ came to celebrate that Last Passover, the LORD's love and faithfulness, did not mean so much to him. After all, he was no sinner. Surely he did not need such love and faithfulness? But they meant everything to Christ. He gives his back to the smiters, embraces the cross, and takes hold of death's cords, not as someone facing an impossible choice, but because he rests everything on this great love and unfailing faithfulness. If the LORD's faithfulness is not forever, if it only gets Jesus up the hill to Calvary, and if he yields up his Spirit only to find God's faithfulness exhausted, then all is lost. But he's a believer. Jesus sings this Psalm with his friends and calls on all nations to praise the LORD, because he believes that the LORD's love and faithfulness is about to invade every nation. In Christ, love's crushing victory will be complete; God will purchase an unfaithful people with his own blood because the LORD's faithfulness never fails.

That is why Paul pictures the risen Christ standing in a great multinational congregation, with the words of this psalm echoing on into eternity. Christ sings to us, and he sings with us. This anthem for a dying lamb has become his anthem once more. The dying lamb stands again (cf. Rev. 5:6) to lead his people in worship. Together, we praise the LORD, for his faithfulness to Jesus, and for his faithfulness to faithless Israel. We would not be here without it. Together, we magnify the LORD, for his love and faithfulness to us and to our fathers. With Christ, we proclaim to all peoples that the LORD is faithful and his love never fails.[3]

Psalm 114 called on the whole earth to tremble in fear at God's saving work for his people. Now Psalm 117 gives the nations the only alternative to dread and trembling before the majesty of God and his exalted Son. The only place where there is no need to tremble before him is in this great congregation where Christ leads his people in praise. For now, for as long as this congregation is still a growing congregation, 'All Welcome' really means all welcome. To join, you need only follow the conductor. Believe his testimony. Listen to his instructions. Follow his directions. Keep in step with him. Let him set the tone of your life. Whoever does that does not just listen to other people sing of his love towards us; they sing with Christ and his people of his love towards us.

Unlike other congregations, this congregation will not disperse. Christ will not sit down and say, 'I don't know.' He is the supreme witness to the love and faithfulness of the LORD. These two words, love and faithfulness, contain a whole gospel. If we could ask Christ, how great is the LORD's love towards us? He would say, 'So great that he will not allow anything to separate us from him.' If we could ask him, how enduring is his

3 Chapter two (p. 31) referred to Scott's study, which may interest anyone keen for a technical discussion that interacts with recent academic literature. His view that 'the Romans become themselves a chorus of psalmists' (93) and that Romans 15 constructs 'an eschatological vision' of increasing grandeur' (95) is appealing, although his claim that Paul's use of Psalms 18 and 117 is sometimes 'entirely heuristic' (113) is not. See Scott, *Hermeneutics of Christological Psalmody in Paul*, 93–132.

faithfulness? He would say, 'So enduring that it will take you to my Father's house, just as it did for me.'

Paul's desire in Romans 15:6 was that God's people would 'glorify the God and Father of our Lord Jesus Christ' with 'one voice.' Christ sings this hymn, and we sing with him, anticipating a day when that will be so. He will take all his loved ones home and gather us together in the new creation. For a little while longer, we must praise the LORD here below, but with the risen Lamb as our leader, even now we raise our voices in the heavenly Jerusalem, and praise the LORD with a great multitude, which no man could number.

8

Save Now!

Psalm 118

'Bind the sacrifice with cords to the horns of the altar' (v. 27). So far as we know, these were the near-final words our Saviour sang as he went out to the place of execution. His heart's focus was in perfect alignment with Psalm 118. These psalms had become his.

That does not mean he could sing easily. One of Dr Johnson's famous quips is that 'when a man knows he is to be hanged... it concentrates his mind wonderfully.' Does it? How could Johnson have known? He died in bed. Perhaps sparkling clarity eludes condemned men as easily as it eludes those who slip away from opioid-induced oblivion into eternal consciousness. And Mary's son was no stoic; his soul was troubled. Yet the focus of this psalm carried him towards the altar.

Psalm 118 has so many scenes that talk of a focus might seem optimistic. On top of that, wider Scripture recalls Psalm 118 so often that it is hard to know what to pinpoint. No Psalm

[1] Give thanks to the LORD for he is good,
for his love endures forever.
[2] Let Israel now say,
his love endures forever.
[3] Let the house of Aaron now say,
his love endures forever.
[4] Let those who fear the LORD now say,
his love endures forever.

[5] In distress I called on the LORD,
the LORD answered me and put me in a broad place.
[6] The LORD is for me,
I will not fear.
What can man do to me?
[7] The LORD is for me as my helper,
and I will see those who hate me.
[8] Better to seek refuge in the LORD than to trust in man.
[9] Better to seek refuge in the LORD than to trust in nobles.
[10] All the nations surrounded me;
in the name of the LORD, I cut them off.
[11] They surrounded me on every side;
in the name of the LORD, I cut them off.
[12] They surrounded me like bees;
they were snuffed out like fire among thorns;
in the name of the LORD, I cut them off.
[13] I was pushed hard so that I was falling,
but the LORD helped me.
[14] The LORD is my strength and my song;
he has become my salvation.
[15] Songs of joy and salvation are in the tents of the righteous.
The right hand of the LORD does valiantly.
[16] The right hand of the LORD exalts;
the right hand of the LORD does valiantly.

[17] I will not die for I will live
and recount the works of the LORD.
[18] The LORD has chastened me severely,
but he has not given me to death.
[19] Open to me the gates of righteousness;
I will enter into them to praise the LORD.

[20] This is the gate of the LORD;
the righteous will enter into it.
[21] I give you thanks
for you answered me and have become my salvation.
[22] The stone that the builders rejected
has become the head cornerstone.
[23] This is what the LORD has done;
it is wonderful in our eyes.
[24] This is the day that the LORD has made;
we will rejoice and be glad in it.
[25] Now LORD, save now.
Now LORD, prosper us now.
[26] Blessed is he who comes in the name of the LORD;
we bless you from the house of the LORD.
[27] The LORD is God; he made light shine on us.
Bind the sacrifice with cords to the horns of the altar.
[28] You are my God and I will sing to you;
my God, I will exalt you.
[29] Give thanks to the LORD for he is good,
for his loving-kindness last forever.

surfaces more often in the New Testament—about 35 times.[1] A casual observer might be forgiven for thinking that as the apostles carried Psalm 118's message into the New Testament, it exploded in their hands sending bits everywhere. The Psalm, however, does have a focus, as well as a coherent and consistent role in the New Testament.

Its focus is not so much an *it* as a *he*—the LORD. Granted, he is the focus of every psalm, but just a glance proves Psalm 118 outstanding. 'The LORD' appears in almost every verse (YHWH and YH 28 times). No other psalm keeps up. Even the runner up, Psalm 119, only uses the LORD's name 24 times. For the psalmist, the LORD is the centre, the beginning and end of salvation. He calls on us to confess that. The identical first and last verses are more than a plea for good etiquette. To 'give thanks to the LORD' will mean proclamatory thanksgiving, which exalts and acclaims the name of the LORD, the character of I AM who I AM—'for he is good.'

Be reticent about this proclamation—'he is good'—and you exclude yourself from the psalmist's company. Those who hesitate, invariably love a world that seeks to define what is good and cannot accept that this adjective got its definition before the world began. No mere creature displays or defines goodness. The LORD does that. I do not determine what is good then judge his goodness. He is its sum and the measure. All that he does is good, from creating first light (Gen. 1:4) to denying or giving spiritual light (Matt. 11:25–6). No good can I receive or possess, except it come from him. In joy and in sorrow, in triumph and in tragedy, in life and in death, every child of God will instinctively say, 'He is good.'

1 Andrew C. Brunson, *Psalm 118 in the Gospel of John* (Tübingen: Mohr Siebeck, 2003), 4. Brunson's work, which began as a doctoral thesis completed under Howard Marshall, offers a useful and comprehensive synthesis of research and commentary on Psalm 118.

That conviction runs through this Psalm, though not as the kind of untested motto one might hear from a group of no-hopers gathered round a life coach, chanting a self-affirming mantra. We speak of tested goodness, as did Jesus Christ when he said, 'No one is good except God alone' (Luke 18:19). Gathered around the Passover table in his company, we should taste and see that the LORD is good. The psalmist's confession should become fuller and richer as we hear Jesus take ownership of this Psalm and himself proclaim that the LORD is good '*for* his love endures for ever' (v. 1).

Generation after generation had proclaimed his goodness in this way, because despite endless provocations, his love had been steadfast, never wholly withdrawn, and always exercised in a way that brought his commitments to pass. This is the covenant love of Psalm 115:1 and 117:2. The Hallel as a whole narrates the story of this love in accounts of the LORD's commitment to his people, individually and corporately. From the outset, the LORD invested everything in Abraham and his children, declaring his willingness to keep his promise even at great cost (Gen. 15:17). As Jesus rises from the Passover table, he must prove that the LORD will not shrink back from that commitment, that he will indeed bear the cost of ensuring that Abraham and his children inherit the new creation (Rom. 4:13). This confession that the LORD is good 'for his loving-kindness endures for ever' therefore also becomes, uniquely for Jesus, a statement of intent. He expects not merely to live out a story of the LORD's love to himself as an individual, but to bring all of God's people into a full and enduring experience of his covenant love.

For Jesus to think like that would not have been to wrest the psalmist's vision from its ancient roots, but rather to see it unobscured by hardened heart or blinded eye. Just as Psalm 115's call to trust in the LORD came to the whole people of God, this proclamation is no less catholic: 'Let Israel…Let the house of Aaron…Let those who fear the LORD, say "His love endures forever"' (vv. 2–4). Preceding psalms anticipated that the people of God would become a great multinational congregation. Psalm 118 shares that hope, drawing together ideas and themes from Psalms 113–117 in a heart-stabilizing focus on the LORD. The identical calls to thanksgiving at the beginning and the end of Psalm 118 are not marks of a backward-looking song. Sandwiched between those two calls is the marrow of a forward-looking Psalm, which calls for more than retrospective thanksgiving.

Perhaps verse 25 best summarizes Psalm 118's goal: 'O LORD, save us.' Famous words. Rather like 'Hallelujah' ('Praise the LORD'), most Christians know the Hebrew behind this heart cry since it is the 'Hosanna' ('Save now') that echoed through the streets of Jerusalem as Jesus entered the city. However we translate it—'Save now!' or 'Save, we pray.'—'Hosanna!' expresses an intense longing. As the psalmist recalls the LORD's past goodness and indestructible love, he exalts and thanks the LORD, begetting an irrepressible longing to taste more of his goodness and love, which in turn breaks out into hosannas.

As with Psalm 116, discussions about the structure of this Psalm soon become more complicated than helpful and more speculative than informative, especially when commentators allow their liturgical imaginations to run ahead of their exegetical discoveries. Even those who detect 'a strongly liturgical character' are forced to confess that 'it cannot be translated into a plausible liturgical sequence.'[2] Yet to bring us to the point of 'Hosanna', Psalm 118 records a certain progress, which Christ himself may have recognised as he made it his song. This chapter will set that out as follows, while highlighting as many New Testament references to Psalm 118 as possible:

2 Zenger, *Psalms 3*, 232.

- First we have an individual testimony (vv. 5–16). The refrain of verses 6–7 states the conviction that energised his advance from a place of distress up to the gates of righteousness: 'The LORD is for me.'
- In verses 17–19 he stands at the gates dismissing all thought of defeat and claiming the right to enter: 'Open to me the gates of righteousness.'
- Finally, in verses 20–28 the gate opens and the psalmist is no longer alone. The testimony of one, his testimony, becomes the testimony of many: 'Blessed is he who comes in the name of the LORD' (v. 26).

'The Lord Is for Me'

His testimony begins, 'In my distress I called on the LORD' (v. 5). Who is this once-distressed supplicant? He is the sufferer of Psalm 116, recalling his grief and pleas to the LORD. He is also a king. Previous chapters mentioned how David produced a songbook designed to bring a people with their king into the LORD's presence. Psalm 118 is a song for a king, not just because it belongs to his songbook, but because it repeats statements from other psalms ascribed to David. Immediately he says, 'he answered by setting me in a broad place' (v. 5) which is what David reports in Psalm 18:19. Then verse 6 restates Psalm 56:11 where David declares his trust in God, and asks, 'What can man do to me?' With such recollections, Psalm 118 draws together the varied experiences of Israel's king to present us with this single testimony.

What do you make of this man? Nations rage against him. Ten thousand troubles surround him. Foes unite in a council of war. Like angry bees, they form a 'shrill, demented choir' around his head (vv. 10–12): 'Kill the king! Annihilate his people!' Though hard pushed, on the brink, and in distress, he says, 'I will not fear… I will look in triumph on my haters' (vv. 6–7). What a man! He keeps his head when all about him are losing theirs. Is that it? Not exactly. He is no superman, but a real, broken, breaking man. Unravelling, yet never unravelled. Falling, yet always standing.

What a man? That's not what he would say, but, 'What a God! What a helper! Yes, I was surrounded. My distress and anguish seemed to last an eternity, but in the end, the power of my enemies died out like fire in a gorse bush: 'I cut them off…I cut them off…I cut them off…' (vv. 10, 11, 12). Because 'the LORD is for me as my helper' (v. 7), 'I cut them off.' And I did it 'in the name of the LORD.' My action and my victory were consistent with his character. When my foes set themselves against me, they set themselves against my God, against his choice, and against his salvation. They set about to cut themselves off even before I cut them off.'

All else is secondary to this: 'The LORD is for me' (vv. 6, 7). The LORD's anointed king may be pulled limb from limb, turned inside out, ruined, mocked, exposed, and abused, but what of it? 'I will not fear. What can man do to me?' (v. 6).

Who is this man who fears no man? But for one thing, he is indistinguishable from humanity: he is a believer—an authentic, unfeigned believer, whose heart is centred on the LORD: 'My head might be a jumble of thoughts and unanswered questions. I don't understand every mystery, but the LORD is for me. I will not fear. What can man do to me?' Childlike trust is still his rule: 'The LORD preserves the simple' (Ps. 116:6). This is the king's testimony, not because he is an anointed king, but because he is a believer.

The testimony belongs to all believers, something that Paul recognises when he recalls verses 6–7: 'If God is for us, who can be against us?' (Rom. 8:31). The test of whether or not that is our testimony touches on our most mundane concerns. You ask yourself some simple questions: Does my heart ache for wealth? Am I covetous like the Pharisees, valuing what God abominates? Am I anxious about money? How would I feel about being left with nothing but food and clothing? Would I, like Paul, be content with that (1 Tim. 6:8)? If anyone thinks such questions trivialise Psalm 118's lofty theme, Hebrews 13:5–6 says otherwise. If 'the LORD is for me' and verses 6–7 are my authentic testimony, that will manifest itself in contentment. If we have such a promise and such a testimony, Hebrews is right; it is the most absurd thing in all the world that we should be discontented, lovers of money.

Although the king's testimony belongs to all believers and touches on such everyday concerns, the king does secure the testimony for them. According to his own report, 'Songs of joy and salvation are in the tents of the righteous' (v. 15). Why joyful songs? It was not always so with Israel (Ps. 106:25). If we hear what they hear, we will not ask 'Why?' Their songs answer the king's song: 'The LORD is my strength and my song; he has become my salvation' (v. 14). It's familiar. Not only have they heard it before, it is their song; Moses gave it to them (Exod. 15:2). Just to hear the king sing these words assures them that his victory is their victory. His exodus is their exodus. When they testify that 'the LORD is for me,' it is not an untested assertion, but a testimony that the king's testimony seals to their hearts. They hear his song and they know that the right hand of the LORD does valiantly. He has triumphed gloriously in and through their king (v. 15–16).

'Open to Me the Gates of Righteousness'

Following the death in July 2011 of Austria-Hungary's last Crown Prince, Otto von Habsburg, his remains were carried to the Imperial Crypt beneath the Capuchin Church in Vienna. As with Otto's ancestors, the Master of Ceremonies knocked on the door three times. In response, the Prior asked, 'Who desires entry?'

'Otto of Austria, once Crown Prince of Austria-Hungary, Royal Prince of Hungary and Bohemia, of Dalmatia, Croatia, Slavonia, Galicia, Lodomerien and Illyria, Grand Duke of Tuscany and Krakow, Duke of Lorraine...Grand Prince of Siebenbürgen...Duke of Upper and Lower Silesia... Etc., etc.'

'We do not know him.'

The Master of Ceremonies knocks three more times.

'Who desires entry?'

'Dr Otto von Habsburg, president and honorary president of the Paneuropean Union, member and former president of the European Parliament...recipient of high civil and ecclesiastical awards, orders, and honors...'

'We do not know him.'

Again the Master of Ceremonies knocks three times.

'Who desires entry?'

'Otto, a mortal, sinful man.'

'So komme er herein!'—'Let him come in!'

As for all his regal forebears, death levelled Otto. Emperors and Princes could only beg for entry to the sanctuary as poor sinners. Whatever they might have done for their subjects in life, in death they were just like them.

Israel's kings faced that humiliation too. Death gathered them to their fathers with no respect for their noble rank. At death's door, even warrior kings in the line of Psalm 118's royal champion lost their conqueror status. They had to plead for asylum from the ravages of Sheol like any son of Adam.

It is at this junction that Psalm 118, like Psalm 117, seems too grand and bold for any king of Israel. There is no cutting him down to size at the door of the sanctuary, but from his own mouth, a dismissal of mortality, 'I shall not die, but live' (v. 17), and a demand for entry, 'Open for me the gates of righteousness; I will enter into them to praise the LORD' (v. 19).

What qualifies him to demand entry at the gates of righteousness? Only righteousness. How can the gatekeepers possibly determine if he has that? What is the test? Life. If the king is alive, if death has not levelled him, he is an immortal, righteous man, not pleading entry to find sanctuary, but demanding entry to provide sanctuary. His victory is his vindication, his deliverance from death, a seal of divine approval, his desire to give thanks, a mark of his single-hearted devotion to the LORD.

We should not think, however, of the righteousness that qualifies him to enter as effortless virtue. The king's distress and manifold difficulties are not forgotten just because he has reached the gates of righteousness. Between his banishment of mortality (v. 17) and his demand for entry (v. 19) comes a statement of the cost: 'The LORD has disciplined me severely' (v. 18). How can it be that the LORD put him through such distress? Because that is how he treats his sons and proves their righteousness. If the king sits pampered on his throne, unwounded and unscarred, how can anyone know if he is the true son whose righteousness entitles him to demand entry? So watch this king, see his Lord seem to get smaller, while his enemies grow stronger. See his God deal with him just as he dealt with all his sons when they toiled in Egypt, and ask, will this son prove himself to be the son that Israel should have been? If the righteous are to share in life and victory, the king must break the cords of death, so that he can say, 'I will not die but live' (v. 17); 'the LORD has not given me over to death' (v. 18). Unless he can say that, his testimony ends at verse 5—in distress, with no song, no joy, no salvation, for him or for anyone else.

If it is true that the LORD hides himself only so that his victory will be more complete in the king's salvation and in the destruction of his enemies, we only get a glimpse of that in the kings of Israel. If he brought forth their righteousness as the light, it seems to have been strangely dimmed. If they were so fully vindicated that their righteousness gave them a right to demand entry into the sanctuary, why did they not live for ever? How come king after king proved himself a mortal, sinful man? Why at this point in Psalm 118, do all Israel's monarchs sound as if they are singing a borrowed song?

It sounds like that because it was a borrowed song, or at least a song that could never be truly theirs until someone would sing it whose righteousness would give him a right to enter the sanctuary, bringing many sons of Israel with him.

On the night of the last Passover, after our LORD Jesus sang this Psalm and went out to pray, he was in great anguish, not least because as he sang with his disciples, he understood that he was not borrowing Psalm 118. He knew that if his testimony ended with verse 5, neither he nor his disciples would ever move beyond distress. As their king, they needed him to gain the victory over an old enemy that no son of David had ever conquered. When the LORD tested David or his sons, they got a graze, or a dark night of the soul. But when the LORD lays the rod upon this Son, it will be no mere corrective or glancing blow. It will be real punishment for real sin—the sin of the men who sing with him, of many who sang before them, and of others who will yet praise the LORD through their testimony.

No wonder Jesus is in agony. Not that he feels it unfair; he came willingly. He is in agony because though he has a little understanding of what he will experience, it will be infinitely worse than anything he could imagine. And if he could not comprehend what he was about to suffer, what are we to make of it? It is true that as with Psalm 116, Psalm 118's life-giving dying becomes the paradigm for every servant of Christ (2 Cor. 6:9), but though the LORD were to discipline me more severely than any of his children, I would still have only a slight apprehension of Christ's agony. The severest chastisement that the LORD visits upon us has no punishment in it; Christ bore it all. But singing Psalm 118, Jesus knows that is what lies ahead: punishment. For him the severe discipline of verse 18, becomes the wages of sin. Death.

So how can he sing, 'I will not die but live…'? The first thing to say is that Jesus' engagement with Psalm 118 began some time before the Last Passover. If Psalm 118 seems to have invaded the New Testament and claimed its territory, that is because Jesus laid claim to Psalm 118. We first become conscious of that in John 11 when Jesus appears at Lazarus' tomb. Having just wept (John 11:35), he is now angry (v. 38). His mood is not mere discomposure, but holy fury—the indignant rage of a battle-ready monarch towards an enemy who seeks his destruction, and the destruction of his people. He comes to the tomb confident that he will look in triumph on his enemies, and say at the end of the battle, 'In the name of the LORD, I cut them off.'

Jesus' address to his Father unveils this mindset. When he says, 'Father, I thank you that you have heard me' (John 11:41), he lets it be known that he expects to achieve something that his psalmist fathers could not achieve when they spoke those words (Ps. 118:21). He wants Martha to know that she got his identity right (John 11:27), and if she wants the complete portrait she will find his likeness in Psalm 118. It is his identity card. His prayer is a statement of faith that his Father will fulfil for him the psalmist's expectations. Hard pressed and in distress, he will still say, 'The LORD is with me'—'I shall not die but live.' What he does now at the tomb will prove it. This is not all about Lazarus; it's all about Jesus, though it will be quite a day for Lazarus. As he emerges from the tomb, still dressed for his own funeral service, the LORD effectively declares to Jesus, 'Yes, I am with you. You shall not die but live.'[3]

What then is the answer to the question, how can he sing, 'I will not die but live…'? Only one way: by faith. When he stands at Lazarus' tomb, he has already taken possession of Psalm 118. It will shape his thoughts when sometime later he

3 For a comprehensive argument see Brunson, *Psalm 118*, 362–77.

goes up from Bethany already prepared for his burial. Because he trusts in the LORD, he will go to die, to do something that is, humanly speaking, foolish. He owns the psalmist's statement, not imagining that he will go Elijah-like to glory, but convinced that what he said to Martha could be said of himself: 'though he die, yet shall he live, and…never die' (John 11:25–6). He believes the LORD will vindicate him as he exhausts death's power; it will go out like a fire among thorns, for himself and for his friends. They will be together again. They will again sing together, 'The LORD is my strength and my song; he has become my salvation.'

'Blessed Is He Who Comes'

As we approach the last part of the Psalm, we move to another stage. The gatekeepers have made their decision, the gate opens, the king enters, and he is no longer alone. Although no one can forget the menace that came before, or the blood-letting that marked the king's path to vindication, a unanimous welcome testifies to a new atmosphere: 'Blessed is he who comes in the name of the LORD' (v. 26).

If in verse 20, by virtue of his righteousness the king is now inside, the gate of the LORD stays open and a throng streams in behind him; the righteous enter in. Who are they? How are they righteous? What qualifies them to enter? The king does. His trauma was for their sake. He fought to set them free. His deliverance is their relief. Their king groaned in his bondage, but the LORD their God heard his cry and stretched out his arm to save the king, so a whole people were liberated to serve the LORD. His testimony has become their testimony. He has gathered them together in the presence of the LORD. The children of Zion rejoice in their king as he leads them in this song: 'I give thanks for you have answered me and have become my salvation' (v. 21).

The first part of the Psalm told us how this came about, but verse 22 puts it in one sentence: 'The stone that the builders rejected has become the cornerstone.' Their king had no place in the grand ambitions of those who surrounded him and sought his destruction. They wanted to build a new world, but not with him. Their rejection thrust him down the road to Sheol. They thought he was gone. But the LORD would get glory over these builders. His anointed, 'the stone the builders rejected,' would become the head cornerstone—a monumental, inconceivable, and impossible reversal. Is it any surprise that the righteous say with their king, 'This is the doing of the LORD' (v. 23)?

It is the LORD's doing, not in part, but in whole. From the king's early distress to his unbearable rejection, from his victory on the battlefield to the gates of righteousness swinging open, it's all the doing of the LORD. This is his way of salvation. He hides himself in a rejected stone until the day comes when he is ready to build an everlasting kingdom upon that stone.

But there is still a question: if what the LORD has done is so impressive, why do we still hear hosannas?—'O LORD, save us; O LORD, grant us success' (v. 25). Surely when the king has returned victorious and he stands within the gates the time for hosannas has passed? But no, they still call out, 'Save now!' Why seek something greater? Even the ancient king shares this yearning: 'Blessed is he who comes in the name of the LORD' (v. 26). The house of the LORD is on the lookout for a new arrival, another king whose life and action will be more consistent with the LORD's character than any other. All things will become clear in his light as he approaches the altar to make his testimony complete (v. 27).

'Who is this?'

Passover after Passover, Jews would sing Psalm 118 looking for this new king. A day came when some of them thought they had found him. Crowds lined the streets shouting, 'Hosanna to the Son of David! Blessed is he who comes in the name of the Lord!' (Matt. 21:9, 15; Mark 11:9–10; John 12:13). There is no doubt what they think of Jesus. To their minds, he is a king and a son of David, who truly comes in the name of the Lord. In their euphoria they even call on the angels to join in: 'Hosanna in the highest!'

But what do the angels think? Are they 'in perfect diapason' with the crowd? Milman's famous Palm Sunday hymn has heaven on the verge of tears: 'The wingéd armies of the sky look down with sad and wondering eyes.' Is that so? They are in the Father's presence, conscious that the Son is going forward to do his will and that they are about to see things they longed to look into (1 Pet. 1:12). If anything, they must be urging him on: 'Go Jesus! Go on to do your Father's will.' Unlike the crowd, however, they have a growing understanding of Christ's mission. The crowd chose the right Psalm, found its owner, and were ready to crown him lord of all, yet as their fervour increased so did their spirit-wrought incomprehension of Jesus' kingship.

None of this took Jesus by surprise. Jerusalem may have been asking, 'Who is this?' (Matt. 21:10), but Jesus has the answer. Even if the crowds have not grasped the message of their chosen Psalm, the Father can still use them as ignorant ministers, whose proclamation will confirm to his Son that he will indeed fulfil the psalmist's expectations. So Jesus continues on the route set out in Psalm 118, striding majestically into the temple to throw out the forex traders and confront compromised clerics.

'The stone the builders rejected'

That confrontation with the chief priests and elders will continue the next day when Jesus returns to teach in the temple courts. Most relevant to Psalm 118 is his retelling of Isaiah's parable of the vineyard (Matt. 21:33–46; Isa. 5:1–7). Initially, Jesus says nothing to unsettle these men. They know the story, and even if Jesus adds something about the murderous tenants, they are ready to answer his question: 'When the owner of the vineyard comes, what will he do to those vinedressers?' (v. 40).

'He will bring those wicked men to a miserable end,' they say, 'and he will lease the vineyard to other tenants…' (v. 41).

What a perfect answer! Such sound men—always ready to make a stand for truth and righteousness.

Except now Jesus has a question for them: 'Have you never read in the Scriptures, "The stone that the builders rejected has become the head cornerstone. This is the work of the Lord and it is marvellous in our eyes"?' (v. 42).

Of course they have read it, but no way will they accept Jesus' interpretation of the Psalm: 'Therefore I say to you, the kingdom of God will be taken from you and given to a people who will produce its fruits' (v. 43). If they know now that Jesus is speaking about them (v. 45), they certainly do not accept that they are the builders of Psalm 118:22.

What will they do? They want to cling to the kingdom, so there is only one thing they can do: seize the heir (v. 46), and after that, cast him outside the city and kill him. In their determination to reject Christ's word, they will fulfil it completely. These wicked tenants think that if they kill the son and heir, they will break the landlord's commitment to his vineyard, but it has the opposite effect. It is not that it becomes a sacred spot for him—'the place where my son died'—the lord of the vineyard has now bound his own future to the prosperity of the vineyard. He sent his son, not with serene detachment from the son's mission, but with such undivided commitment to his success that even if his son should appear to fail, he will make sure he brings fruit home.

What does that mean? It means that 'the stone the builders rejected has become the chief cornerstone.' Humanly speaking, that is nonsense. How can it be that once the builders have done their work, that a stone cast away as rubble becomes the key stone in the building? It can only mean that what they have built is not what the Lord wanted. They had his instructions and they were fastidious with the measurements, but they threw away that stone without which the building cannot stand, so it will all come tumbling down.

But the Lord himself will recover that stone and build again. The rejected stone and the slaughtered son are two ways of describing the same thing. So if the rejected stone becomes the cornerstone, Jesus was saying that the murdered son would become the cornerstone of this nation to whom the kingdom of God would be given. And if he will become the cornerstone of that nation, then he must live again. When the son dies outside the vineyard, by some great paradox the vineyard's most tender shoot will produce its first real fruit.

This exposition of Psalm 118 was not just a means for Jesus to condemn the religious establishment. It was his spiritual food and drink, an understanding of the Psalm that had been growing in his mind and strengthening his faith as he drew closer to his final ordeal. He knows that Psalm 118 was intended for him and that he must make it a song for many others. That means he must suffer and enter into battle, be rejected by men and become a stranger to his mother's sons. He must die. But, 'the LORD is for me,' he can say (v. 6), so 'I will not die but live' (v. 17). The rejected son will become the cornerstone.

'You will not see me again, until you say...'

Jesus has not yet finished with the scribes and Pharisees, or with Psalm 118. His final interaction with them will be an excoriating exposure of their hypocrisy (Matt. 23:1–36). Yet his stern words are not the pronouncements of an impassive scrutineer, but of someone who is, has been, and will be, profoundly affected by the sin he condemns. That is why he breaks into a lament, which is not an expression of momentary distress, but of what he is and who he is. He mourns over what they have done and are about to do, not out of self-pity, but in anguish at what their sin will to do them. 'How often' he wanted to gather Jerusalem's children together, 'as a hen gathers her chicks under her wings' (v. 37). This is not an expression merely of his human desire; Jesus laments as Emmanuel, the 'God with us' of Matthew 1:23, under whose wings this rebellious people—the wicked tenants—could always find shelter (Ps. 36:7; 91:4). But they 'were not willing' (v. 37).

That unwillingness is an incomprehensible tragedy. It has consequences: 'Behold, your house is left to you desolate,' he says (v. 38). What house? The house of which Jesus had said a little earlier, 'My house shall be called a house of prayer' (Matt. 21:13), and which he also called, 'My Father's house' (John 2:16). This holy temple had become the place of which God said, 'there I will meet with you' (Exod. 25:22). No longer. It is not now 'my house,' but 'your house.' Not the Father's house, but their house. Not a glory-filled tabernacle, but a fetid den of religious iniquity. With these words, Jesus confirms the transfer of God's house to their possession. All the ministrations of priests and Levites now become 'mockeries.' Shortly the temple veil will be rent in two; it will be as if a sign now hangs over the temple, which reads, 'Condemned Building: Do not enter.' Under the pastorate of priests and Pharisees, the service of the temple has so spectacularly failed that it is now absolutely useless.

What does that mean for those who remained committed to it? Jesus answers that in his final quotation from Psalm 118: 'I say to you, you will not see me again, until you say, "Blessed is he who comes in the name of the Lord!"' (Matt. 23:39). In other words, his interaction with them is over; he will not return to them. He certainly will not return to the temple to preach and teach. That house will not even know the mercy of his whip driving out its abusers.

'A time will come,' Jesus says to them, 'when you acknowledge me as the suffering king of Psalm 118. You will confess that I am the stone that became the cornerstone, and you will recognise this day as the day that the Lord had made. The benediction that you wished to deny the children of Jerusalem when they shouted, '"Blessed is he who comes in the name of the Lord," will become your irresistible, lamenting confession.'

With that, the day of salvation for old Jerusalem and all that it represents is past. The first words of Matthew 24 remove any doubt: 'Then Jesus went out and departed from the temple.' What has Jesus done? This was more than a departure. It was an act of war—something the king had to do before he could enter the gates of righteousness. He said, 'They surrounded me on every side; in the name of the LORD, I cut them off.' And now he has done it. His departure was a cutting off of those who killed the prophets and who will now kill him. The circumcised have become the uncircumcised, which will be confirmed absolutely when Jesus himself is cut off in death. In any case, Jesus has departed. Emmanuel is gone. God with us—never again.

'Marvellous in our eyes'

Jesus' public ministry through the medium of Psalm 118 is now over, but the way it shaped his interactions with his Father, with those at Lazarus' tomb, with the crowds, and with old Jerusalem, will remain with him as he goes to sit at the table with his friends one more time. As they sing Psalm 118, he will sing knowing he is on the way to die, knowing he will not just be laid on the altar, but bound and fastened like no other sacrifice, bound to face a double-death, a first and second death combined. A plague of darkness will fall over his life, so thick that even nature will be compelled to acknowledge it (Matt. 27:45), but through his darkness, the LORD makes his light shine upon us (v. 27), so that the people of God will always have light where they live (Exod. 10:22–3).

If Psalm 118 has helped Jesus walk this far, its promise will also strengthen him as he makes the final sacrifice. Should anyone question his ownership of Psalm 118, or demand to know how he expects to live and to enter the gate of the LORD, he could ask them a familiar question: 'Have you never read in the Scriptures: "The stone which the builders rejected has become the cornerstone; this was the Lord's doing, and it is marvellous in our eyes"?'

There is no other word for it, but 'marvellous' or 'wonderful'. How marvellous that God should have inspired this psalmist to compose a song for a later age, for a people yet unborn, and for a king whose beauty and perfection his eyes had not yet seen. How wonderful that when the king came into this world he came willingly, taking possession of this Psalm, embracing its pain and rejection, believing its promises and walking by faith. How marvellous that the LORD made our rejected brother the cornerstone and set us upon him as living stones (Eph. 2:19–21; 1 Pet. 2:4–5). How wonderful that although it is all so marvellous it is not too wonderful or too marvellous for God's children to understand (Deut. 30:11; Ps. 131:1). 'This is the day that the LORD has made; we will rejoice and be glad in it' (v. 24).

As with other Psalms in the Hallel, the New Testament is not content to leave Psalm 118 with the old Jerusalem, it calls upon us to carry the rejoicing and the gladness of the day that the LORD has made forward to the day of vindication for the Lamb and his bride (Rev. 19:7–8). This recalling of Psalm 118 continues an earlier reference to the Hallel (Rev. 19:1–5; p. 81), yet Scripture's final allusion puts the Psalm's vision in even sharper focus. The king's demand, 'Open to me the gates of righteousness' (v. 19), is answered not in old Jerusalem, but in the new. When the righteous enter into the gate of the LORD (v. 20), they find themselves not in the temple courts, but in a city without a physical temple. In Revelation 22:14, the gates, 'which the Psalmist asked to be opened for him'[4] are open to

4 Bede, *Revelation*, 284.

the righteous. Not one of them has been given over to death. The gates are open to them so that they may enter in and claim the right to life. Why has this right to enter and to live been bestowed upon once-mortal, sinful men? Because the King of glory has already entered in. Thus his testimony has become theirs: 'I shall not die but live and recount the works of the LORD' (v. 17).

Hosanna!

As we come to the end of the Hallel, John's apocalyptic unveiling of its goal should only intensify our yearning for its fulfilment. 'Hosanna! Save now,' is a cry that belongs to this age, not because we look for another king, but because we wait for the same king, the same Lord Jesus, to come again in the name of the LORD.

There is of course an alternative. The warning notes of Psalm 114 and 115 echo even into Psalm 118. Stand with the builders who rejected Jesus, stumble over him and his claims, and he will warn you as he warned them, 'Whoever falls on this stone will be dashed to pieces, and when it falls on anyone, it will crush him' (Matt. 21:44).

The Hallel leaves a question with every reader or singer of its songs in this age: What would you have the king do for you? Crush you or save you? He is coming in the name of the LORD. Reject him now and he will crush you. Cry, 'Hosanna; Lord, save now!' and he will save you.

'Give thanks to the LORD for he is good, for his love endures for ever' (v. 1, 29).

9

O Lord, Open Our Lips

A broken man once pleaded, 'O Lord, open my lips and my mouth shall declare your praise' (Ps. 51:15). His plea resonated so deeply with Christians that it became a principle petition in many liturgies. He waited for the sin-bearer that they remembered, yet the Old Testament worship-leader and New Testament worshippers sensed the same deep need for a heart-cleansing, spirit-renewing work of God, which would bring with it joy of salvation, nobility of spirit, and assurance of pardon, constraining them to use their tongues to sing of his righteousness. But fallen worshippers soon discover that what constrains may not empower or break the seal upon their lips. Thus, penitential David's plea became a universal orison: 'O Lord, open thou our lips and our mouth shall shew forth thy praise.'

What does it take for our lips to be opened? Specifically, what does it take for our lips to be opened so that we declare God's praise through the Psalms? In chapter two I mentioned Wright's 'attempt to reverse those trends' that have seen large parts of the Western church either stop using the Psalms, or reduce them to liturgical 'filler'.[1] He aims to help Christians rejoin a trans-millennial, trans-cultural chorus:

> The Psalms offer us a way of joining in a chorus of praise and prayer that has been going on for millennia and across all cultures. Not to try to inhabit them, while continuing to invent non-psalmic "worship" based on our own feelings of the moment, risks being like a spoiled child who, taken to the summit of Table Mountain with the city and the ocean spread out before him, refuses to gaze at the view because he is playing with his Game Boy.[2]

Yet inhabiting the Psalms demands effort; anyone who wants to do that must 'try'. For Wright, that meant, amongst other things, developing a five-a-day habit as a student.[3] For all of us, it will mean striving for understanding, not only of the Psalms in their original context, but of their fulfilment in the life of Christ and their role in the New Testament. Spoiled Christians may judge that too much trouble, especially if they are engrossed in their games. In that case, their lips will never be opened. To shun understanding is beneath humanity (Ps. 32:8–9; 49:20), to say nothing of Christianity. No one who wants to know Christ better can be content with ignorance.

If the LORD will open our lips to declare his praise, he will use the same means that he used to open Christ's lips. Though sin had neither sealed the lips of our unfallen second Adam, nor darkened his understanding, his lips would not be opened for the ultimate declaration of praise until he had been delivered from the burden of bearing other people's sin. To get to that point, he had to hear the Word of God, as morning by morning his Father awakened his ear to hear, teaching him

1 Wright, *Case for the Psalms*, 1

2 Ibid., 6.

3 Ibid., 171–196.

even through those whose understanding would never match his own. But as he listened and questioned, as he internalized the laws of Moses and the predictions of prophets, the Holy Spirit filled his ready mind with a knowledge of his person and work, which prepared him to step into the role that David and his sons could not fulfil. As he takes ownership of David's hymn book, the Spirit teaches him more about himself and his Father's will, opening his lips to declare his praise to his disciples, until at their final gathering, and after their last song, the Lamb knows the time for silence has come, but that the LORD will again open his lips to declare his praise in the great congregation.

By the same means, the LORD opens our lips. Through the same Word of God and the same Spirit of Truth, we gain understanding that equips us to declare his praise. Yet it is not just a matter of means, or of saying we need to do what Jesus did. The opening of our lips to praise comes through knowing Jesus Christ, and perhaps we only know him as well as we know and understand his interaction with Scripture. If his use of Scripture seems to me incomprehensible, or even wrong, how well do I know him? If I love him, I will yearn to understand what he might have thought, and how he might have felt, as he sang those Psalms. If I want my lips to be opened to declare his praise, I will, at his prompting, want to sing his songs with him now.

None of this is meant to suggest that we can have as full a grasp of the Psalms as did Jesus Christ. It is not even meant to suggest that his own understanding was absolutely complete. If it were, he would not have asked, 'Why?' (Ps. 22:1; Matt. 27:46). But his knowledge gives him sufficient grounds for faith to believe that his Father will vindicate him and give him the victory, even in incomprehension. Though sinful lusts could not seize an opportunity to transform his temptations into the unbelief of fallen men, by the Spirit, his faith withstood assaults that no wretched man would ever face. The triumph of his faith—his conviction that he stooped down low to raise the poor, that the earth would tremble at his presence, that the place of silence would not hold him, that he would walk in the land of the living, that he would call all nations to praise, and that his rejection would become the cornerstone of the new creation—was not an easy victory that makes our victory look difficult, but an unequalled contest that makes our believing the lesser challenge. Inspired poets set out his life-paradigm and recorded divine promises to sustain him. He believed, having yet to test these promises. We believe, having seen him put them fully to the test and shown their worth. As we exercise faith in that same Word by that same Spirit, our God's 'Yes' becomes our 'Amen.' He opens our lips to declare his praise.

Will our understanding of Christ's life with the Psalms, and of their fulfilment in him, ever be complete? Will he himself ever fully understand? When we sing the Hallel by sight and not by faith (pp. 83–7, 125–6), will we capture the panorama in a snap? Will we 'have at once all the glory of what he is… presented to us in one view, all comprehended by us at once'?[4] Or might it be 'that the full glory of Christ remains a mystery even to Himself'?[5] Perhaps both statements are true. We will have no painful sense of inadequacy in our understanding. Nor will he. It will be no slow dawn, but instant day. Yet in that pure light we shall see more light. When by the fiery sea, saints' lips are opened to sing the song of Moses, which is also the song of the Lamb (Rev. 15:3), in whatever sense their knowledge is complete, their wonder and insight is ever increasing. Every child of Adam, who hears their King call them to praise in the new creation, will from opened lips make ancient Hallelujahs a new song to the LORD and to the Lamb.

4 Owen, *Glory of Christ*, 215.

5 Donald MacLeod, *From Glory to Golgotha* (Fearn: Christian Focus Publications, 2002), 7.